FILIPPA-K.COM

Filippa K

PARACHUTE

Swedish jewelry tradition meets modern Scandinavian design

The Swedish watch brand Mockberg finds its inspiration in the traditions of Swedish craftsmanship. The name itself comes from Mockberget, a small mountain near Lake Siljan in Dalarna, in the middle part of Sweden. Dalarna, which means "the valleys" in Swedish, has long been the home of Sweden's jewelry makers. In its SS18 collection, Mockberg focusses on bright yet modest colors.

For more information visit mockberg.com

OUR FAVORITE DESIGN
WORLDWIDE SPOTS OF THE MOMENT
DESIGN TRENDS
DESIGNER PORTRAITS
VISITS TO WORKSHOPS
INTERVIEWS OF MODERN TRIBES
INSPIRING INTERIORS
ESCAPE NOTEBOOK

— "Welcome to the cabinet of curiosities called MilK Decoration"

milkdecoration.com

NEW PERSPECTIVES ON SCANDINAVIAN DESIGN

MUUTO

HERSCHEL
SUPPLY
TRAVEL

WELLTRAVELLED
herschel.com

KINFOLK

FOUNDER & CREATIVE DIRECTOR
Nathan Williams

EDITOR-IN-CHIEF
Julie Cirelli

EDITOR
John Clifford Burns

BRAND DIRECTOR
Amy Woodroffe

DESIGN DIRECTOR
Alex Hunting

ART DIRECTOR
Kevin Pfaff

CEO
Peter Hildebrandt

COMMUNICATIONS DIRECTOR
Jessica Gray

CASTING DIRECTOR
Sarah Bunter

SALES & DISTRIBUTION DIRECTOR
Frédéric Mähl

ADVERTISING DIRECTOR
Pamela Mullinger

COPY EDITOR
Rachel Holzman

BUSINESS OPERATIONS MANAGER
Kasper Schademan

STUDIO MANAGER
Aryana Tajdivand-Echevarria

EDITORIAL ASSISTANTS
Lena Hunter
Cecilie Jegsen
Garett Nelson

CONTRIBUTING EDITORS
Michael Anastassiades
Jonas Bjerre-Poulsen
Andrea Codrington Lippke
Ilse Crawford
Margot Henderson
Leonard Koren
Hans Ulrich Obrist
Amy Sall
Matt Willey

ILLUSTRATION
Chidy Wayne

STYLING, HAIR & MAKEUP
Ignacio Alonso
Line Bille
Bethany Brill
Brit Cochran
Mascha Meyer
Jonathan Sanchez
Ianthe Wright

PRODUCTION & SET DESIGN
Sven Alberding
Kindall Almond
Sue Choi
Barbara Gullstein
Jordy Huinder
Abel Sloane
Kingsley Tao

PUBLICATION DESIGN
Alex Hunting

CROSSWORD
Molly Young

WORDS
Alex Anderson
Ellie Violet Bramley
Matt Castle
Joan Didion
Djassi DaCosta Johnson
Charmaine Li
Harriet Fitch Little
Jessica Lynne
David Plaisant
Tristan Rutherford
Charles Shafaieh
Peter Smisek
Haydée Touitou
Pip Usher
Priscilla Ward

PHOTOGRAPHY
Berta Bernad
Kira Bunse
Claire Cottrell
Greg Cox
Ralph Crane
Jean-Claude Deutsch
Alfred Eisenstaedt
Lucia Fatima
Osma Harvilahti
Cecilie Jegsen
Billy Kidd
Annie Lai
Katie McCurdy
Aida Muluneh
Hasse Nielsen
Noell Oszvald
Alexander Rotondo
Jean-Claude Sauer
Marsý Hild Þórsdóttir
Claus Troelsgaard
Pierre Vauthey
Pia Winther
Alexander Wolfe
Ruby Woodhouse

ISSUE 27

info@kinfolk.com
www.kinfolk.com

Published by Ouur Media
Amagertorv 14, Level 1
1160 Copenhagen, Denmark

The views expressed in Kinfolk magazine are those of the respective contributors and are not necessarily shared by the company or its staff.

SUBSCRIBE
Kinfolk is published four times a year. To subscribe, visit *kinfolk.com/subscribe* or email us at *info@kinfolk.com*

CONTACT US
If you have questions or comments, please write to us at *info@kinfolk.com*. For advertising inquiries, get in touch at *advertising@kinfolk.com*

HI MISTER ED!

WOLF&RITA
SS18

"All I wanted to do was to be loved and to love."
BENJAMIN CLEMENTINE — P.48

Photograph: Katie McCurdy

QUALITY AS A TOP PRIORITY

Erik Jørgensen Møbelfabrik was founded in 1954 in Svendborg, Denmark, by saddlemaker and upholsterer Erik Jørgensen. Erik Jørgensen's collection consists of well-known classics from Hans J. Wegner and Poul M. Volther as well as new furniture produced in collaboration with upcoming designers.

We aim to produce furniture that lasts. Not only for use but also to beautify our surroundings, and open our eyes to new ways of seeing and making furniture. A passion for design and good craftsmanship is what characterizes Erik Jørgensen Møbelfabrik.

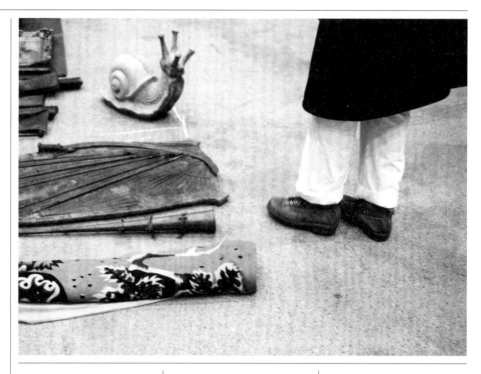
"I'm selling a fantasy image of Paris to the world."
RAMDANE TOUHAMI — P.152

tf

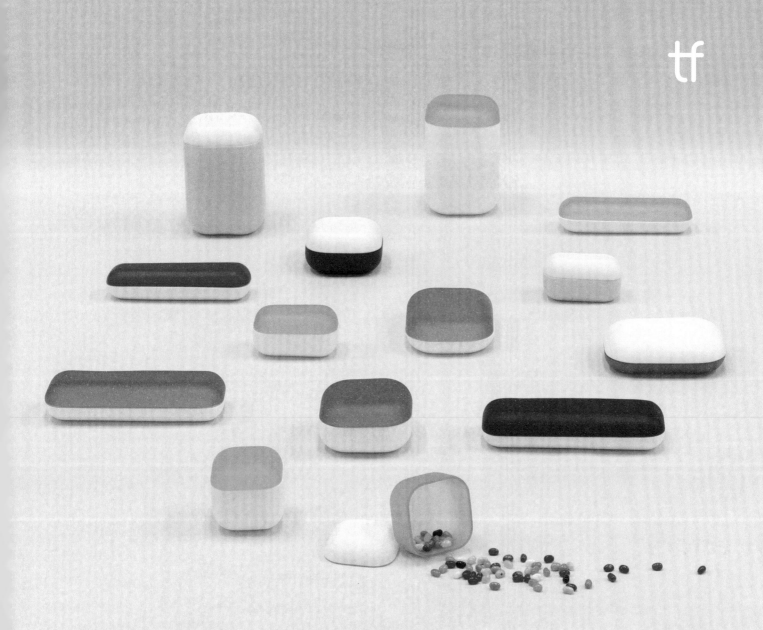

S P R I N G   2 0 1 8

www.apuntob.it

21 — 42

Starters

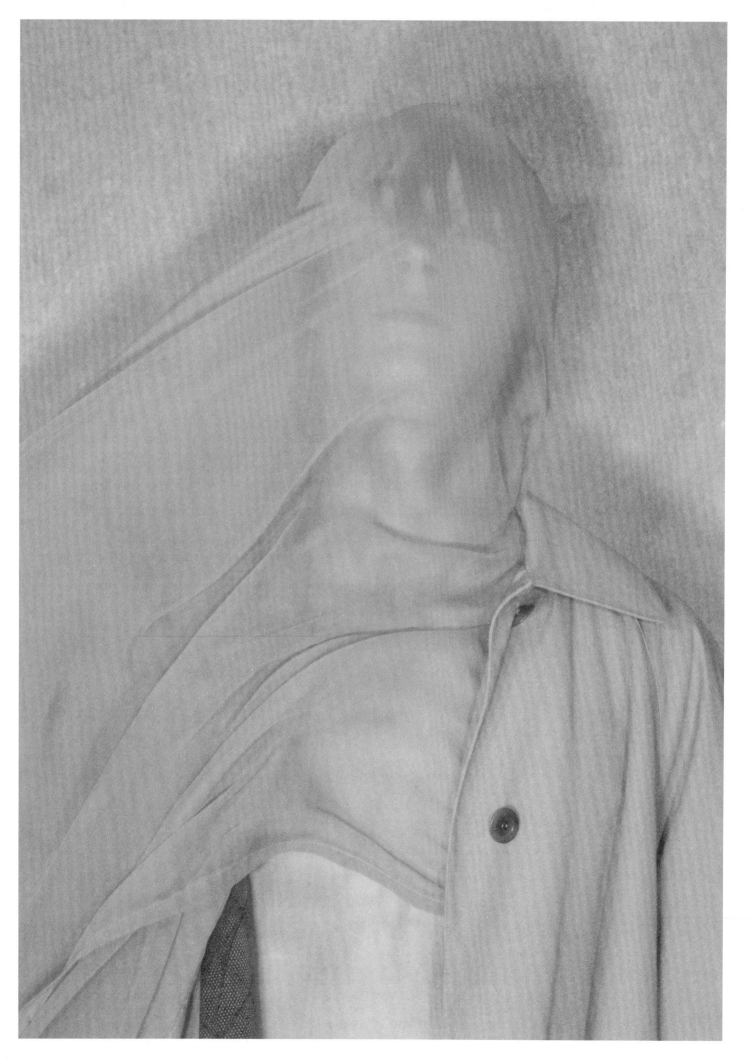

Photograph: Claus Troelsgaard, Hair and Makeup: Line Bille. Overleaf: Photograph by Billy Kidd

ALEX ANDERSON
On Self-Sacrifice

A cost-benefit analysis of altruism.

Most days present us with opportunities to commit minor altruistic acts, small choices to forgo an advantage for the good of someone else—waking early to make the coffee, standing to let an elderly person sit on a crowded train, slowing down to allow another car to merge onto the highway. These moments of mild self-sacrifice seem like the right thing to do, but often defy logical analysis on reflection. After my good deed, I arrive at work a bit drowsy, a little footsore, or a few seconds late, to what end? In a personal cost-benefit calculation, each act exacts a price but rarely seems to yield a direct, tangible dividend.

If these acts are "right," *why* are they right? This question becomes more profound when the sacrifices increase, when choosing selfless actions might impact our own welfare or health—as when donating heavily to a cause or rescuing an injured motorist from a burning car. Deeper consideration of why such acts are right suggests that they aren't just inherently good; they also yield hidden benefits, such as a sense of personal wholeness, mutual regard or social approval.

While individual acts of selflessness might be costly, making a habit of acting selflessly yields cumulative rewards. American journalist and writer Joan Didion hints at this in a thoughtful description of self-sacrifice, which, she says, "is the sense that one lives by doing things one does not particularly want to do, by putting fears and doubts to one side, by weighing immediate comforts against the possibility of larger, even intangible, comforts." She suggests that the daily succession of simple, inconvenient choices—to work a little harder, to take small risks, to help out despite the hassle—is likely to lead toward better things.

We might worry that the cumulative cost is hardly worth what seems an uncertain, distant gain. In fact, these acts bring about their own benefits over time, in what psychologist Howard Rachlin calls "highly valued patterns of behavior." He explains that we derive deep personal satisfaction from the consistency of our actions, especially when we and others perceive them to be ethical or right. These patterns, not the specific moments of self-sacrifice, make us happy and define who we are.

Even so, it seems a little jaded to cast our day-to-day acts of self-sacrifice as a steady grind toward some future reward. It isn't all short-term cost and long-term gain. When our acts of self-sacrifice benefit someone else, we naturally take pleasure in their reaction. According to psychologists George Ainslie and Nick Haslam, built-in neurophysiological mechanisms connect us deeply with each other. They explain that "vicarious feeling of other people's emotions is a primary good" and that it is a compelling reward for altruistic action. Empathy yields immediate emotional returns when we make others happy or relieve their suffering.

Sympathetic bystanders who witness an act of kindness or a heroic rescue also share emotions of happiness and relief and reward the act with admiration. This is particularly true if they see it as part of a larger pattern of altruism (rather than as a single act driven by some self-serving motive). While the habitually altruistic might brush off public admiration, it feels good anyway, and it builds social capital.

We know that leaders who act selflessly inspire not just admiration, but also cooperation. Researchers at the Rotterdam School of Management have shown that business leaders who engage "in self-sacrificial behavior are considered more charismatic, effective and legitimate." Employees reward their self-sacrifice with "trust, cooperation, and improved performance." This seems almost obvious: It is far easier to work for a generous boss than one who is self-absorbed, especially after arriving at the office drowsy and footsore from our own selfless acts.

Individual acts of self-sacrifice may just seem like the right thing to do, and they usually are. But the key is to make altruism a lifetime habit. Selflessness helps us to identify and connect with other people, and it boosts our ability to work well with others.

The etiquette of death.

CHARMAINE LI

Good Grief

Avoid the impulse to give a grieving person space. Reach out without the expectation of a prompt reply, says etiquette expert Margaret Shepherd.

When it comes to acknowledging death, we're often puerile and ill at ease. Despite being desperate to console a loved one, we find ourselves anxious and stammering for the right words.

Margaret Shepherd, author of *The Art of Civilized Conversation: A Guide to Expressing Yourself with Style and Grace*, believes talking about death is still taboo in Western society because many people have never had to deal with it directly. "It happens in a hospital or when they're not there, so they're talking about something they don't know about personally and it makes them uncertain," she explains in a call from her home in Boston.

For Shepherd, sitting by her mother's side while she died took the mystery and eeriness out of death, and helped her get over the fear of talking about the subject. Not everyone will have that particular experience, but nearly everyone can gain understanding by contemplating mortality. There are a range of practices in Buddhism called *maranasati* that involve meditating on death and impermanence. You can help assuage your fears by reflecting on the idea that while death is a given, its timing is uncertain. German philosopher Martin Heidegger argued that individuals had to face the reality of death in order to live authentic lives. A regular reminder that each day could be your last can unveil a holistic view on life and a vivid awareness of what you see, say or do.

Although grief is a natural phase of life that each of us will experience at one time or another, it's still challenging every time you encounter it. You might shy away from the recently bereaved for fear of not knowing what to say, but Shepherd tells me it's important to reach out as soon as you know about a death to let someone know you're thinking of them—whether that be through a text message, phone call, email or handwritten note.

"You say, 'I'm sorry.' 'I'm so sorry to hear it.' 'We're thinking of you.' 'This must be hard for you,'" she advises. But don't leave it at that. Tell them you're there to listen and help if they need, while keeping in mind that it might be hard for the grieving person to meet face-to-face. "Whatever you do," she adds, "don't downplay what happened to them or be indirect and euphemistic about it."

TIME AFTER TIME

by Garett Nelson

From desk clocks to wristwatches, objects devoted to keeping time are increasingly being replaced by the omnipresent screen. And while new technology provides ease and efficiency in its multifunctionality, it can leave us longing for the real thing. Here, to help curb the effects of screen fatigue and the obsessive impulse to check phones, is a selection of some of our favorite artfully designed timepieces: George Nelson's Tripod Clock (top), Schoolhouse Electric's Flip Clock (middle) and Arne Jacobsen's Station Clock (bottom).

MATT CASTLE

On Measuring Pain

How much can something hurt?

Pain is hard to pin down. It can be sharp, dull, burning, constricting, throbbing or colicky. It can be acute or chronic. For many, there is no close correlation between physical damage and the degree of pain experienced. There is an inherently subjective aspect to pain: Mood, attitudes and external events can all influence how it is perceived. It is even possible to endure agony from a part of the body that no longer exists, as amputees suffering from phantom limb pain can attest. Compounding this, we frequently talk about emotional pain in the same breath as the physical variety, making it all too easy for us to dismiss pain as "all in the mind."

It's hardly surprising that measuring pain is tricky business. Pain specialists are usually careful to avoid being judgmental, often recording patients' own descriptions of their symptoms. Despite this, numerical scores remain a necessary, if intrinsically flawed, element of pain assessment. The commonly used numerical rating scale (NRS) allows patients to score their pain between zero and 10—with zero being no pain, and 10 being the worst pain imaginable. Of course, whether that person has experienced childbirth—or gout, kidney stones or cluster headaches—will likely skew their personal pain calibration scale. And for some, the worst thing about their pain is not so much its magnitude, but its relentlessness.

Accurate quantification may never be possible, but research continues to advance our understanding of pain perception. In 2011, Ethan Kross and colleagues published a study comparing the brain activity of participants receiving two different stimuli. First they were shown photographs of their ex-partner (all participants were selected on the basis of having recently ended a relationship). Then an uncomfortably hot "thermode end-plate" was applied to their left forearm. In both instances, similar brain areas were activated. The study's conclusion: "Social rejection shares somatosensory representations with physical pain." So, both physical and emotional pain are objectively detectable phenomena. And they appear to be pretty much the same thing, neurologically speaking. So while we can't fully understand someone else's pain, we can agree that whether it's "in the mind" or in the body, it can really hurt.

Left photographs: Pia Winther, Right photograph: Lucia Fatima

Photography: Corbis/VCG/Getty Images

ALEX ANDERSON

Dead of Night

Fey and fearful: the superstitions of the witching hour.

Compline was the hour for nightly prayer, marking the end of the day for monks of the Middle Ages. Normally involving meditation on death, it initiated the hours of dark and silence—a perilous time. As monks, priests and bishops drifted to sleep, their authoritative prayers faded and spiritual protections weakened.

And so, on their knees in darkened bedrooms, people intoned an ancient hymn, begging for divine protection: "From evil dreams defend our sight,/ From fears and terrors of the night; / Tread underfoot our deadly foe/ That we no sinful thought may know." Continuing the bedtime litany, they recited yet more fearful prayers, urging themselves to "be sober, be vigilant, because your adversary the devil is prowling around like a roaring lion, seeking for someone to devour." Hardly restful words to drift off with.

In the darkening night, the faithful and the superstitious lay awake and envisioned freewheeling devilry, unchecked by the dozing pious. The witching hour— from midnight until 3:00 a.m. —was when spirits and spells be-

came their most potent. Then at 3:00 a.m., during the devil's hour, Satan emerged transcendent to mock the Holy Trinity and Christ's 3:00 p.m. crucifixion—and to devour unprotected souls.

Supernatural threats aside, the darkest hour of night is no time for humans to be about. We are physiologically ill-suited to nocturnal pursuits. Lions, like other feline predators, have night vision nearly 10 times better than ours, a stealthy tread and a huge appetite. Owls see in the gloom one hundred times better than we do, cockroaches ten thousand times. Bats get by fine without any light at all.

Even for those tucked safe in bed, 3:00 a.m. can be devilish. Melatonin levels peak, carrying sleepers into the strangest and most vivid of the night's dreams. Body temperature drops, pulse slows, blood pressure weakens. If you happen to die at night, research suggests it will happen between 3:00 and 5:00 a.m. But when it's time for the monks to sing lauds in the moments before dawn, the light rises, our eyes adjust and body warms, and the last fears of the night evaporate with the mist.

A conversation with a New York psychoanalyst.

Jamieson Webster

Photograph: Katie McCurdy, Styling: Kindall Almond, Hair & Makeup: Brit Cochran

Psychoanalytic terms—including such pop favorites as "repression," "Oedipal complex" and "narcissism"—are part of the vernacular, and yet psychoanalysis as a profession remains maligned. But analyst Jamieson Webster, who practices in Manhattan's SoHo neighborhood, is fine with that. A professor at the New School as well as a cultural critic, Webster agrees with Freud, who believed that since psychoanalysis concerns things that make us uncomfortable, it will always face resistance. Here, Webster talks about the benefits of forgetting, the myths about psychoanalysis, and how difficult listening is for all of us.

What drew you to psychoanalysis? I think being sick is the only reason people become analysts. I read Freud early, and when I was 14, I wanted to be a parapsychologist, which was about hauntings and the uncanny. The minute I got to New York, I found an analyst, but really, I was in trouble. You spend a lot of time in analysis wrestling with your issues, and then have to figure out if you want to become an analyst because you truly want to help people. Analysis confronts the altruistic impulse as false. It isn't going to fulfill the wishes that made you go into this in the first place; it's going to make you stare at those wishes in their unfulfillability. At that point, you must determine if you still want to do this work.

Like an artist, that work involves bringing details to the surface. The power of certain painters—when they create a work of art—is that they make something visible that wasn't visible before. Psycho-analysis does the same thing by highlighting an off-center detail, something that sticks out, and pushing it back into the center for the patient. Dreams often have drama, but there's frequently a little detail that unravels their meaning. That's why we should read literature more than we should study neuroscience. Patients are strange, and when you break through them, there's all this crazy material but also something wonderful.

There's a trend—in creative writing courses, in media campaigns —to "tell your story." How is that different than what happens in your sessions? There's an entitled impulse that people believe they have a story to tell. But it's very difficult to tell your story, and the story you tell is always a lie. You must work in peculiar ways to discover that your conscious narrative is wrong and then find the other meanings. I would have been terrified if I had to tell my own story. Psychoanalysis is more about breaks in the narrative than the narrative itself. Maybe a different story can emerge after breaking something down. I understand the impulse in identity politics, about how your narrative has been written out of history, but that's a fight for power. There's something dangerous about confusing identity and power. Psychoanalysis is about who we are, and there's no power there. What you end up saying in analysis is a deeply disempowered story.

If you're writing your own story, you're not listening. Are we experiencing a crisis of listening? I think so. Take psychoanalytic training: five to six years of graduate school and a minimum five to six years of analytic training. That's 12 years of learning how to listen! Realizing how hard it is makes me very pessimistic about what's possible outside this office. When listening is this hard, I get scared when I think about real situations that have real consequences. Most of the time when you're in a conversation with others, you're filling in your own story. Usually, we talk about safe spaces for speaking, but I think it would be much better to have safe spaces to listen.

Psychoanalysis is not about morality, and it's very hard to listen without morality. We're returning to morality today—there's outrage on every side—and while there are things to be angry about, we need to get morality out of the picture before we can really listen. It's judgment, usually reactionary and immediate, that typically comes from your own self. You're persecuting yourself for something about which you feel guilty.

One myth about psychoanalysis is that repression is terrible. We live in an age where, because of technology, nothing is lost. Are there benefits of forgetting? Forgetting allows us to restart. It creates the unconscious, which gives us a hidden reservoir to put things in, to which later we can return. Patients in their most anxious states are trying to keep everything right there in front of them instead of putting it all back into the container, letting it come back in due course, and establishing their own unique rhythm of forgetting, remembering and having things come to consciousness. Without repression, we'd all be delirious and insane.

"Forgetting allows us to restart... Without repression, we'd all be delirious and insane."

Webster regularly contributes to *The Guardian* with psychoanalytical musings on sexting politicians and presidents with personality disorders.

ZINOVATNAYA

by Ellie Violet Bramley

From faded 1970s mustard tones to seaside pistachios, forest greens, deep night-sky blues and urgent reds, the color combinations of Russian designer Daria Zinovatnaya are bold and unusual. "When I use color in my work," she says, "it comes alive. I wish that people were not so afraid of using lots of color." The work of Zinovatnaya's eponymous St. Petersburg studio extends to industrial, furniture and interior design, and has been commissioned for apartments, hotels and restaurants from Russia to the United States. Born in Crimea, Zinovatnaya grew up admiring 20th-century design. Now, at 25, she is still enraptured by the work of Italian architect and designer Ettore Sottsass; in her work you can see reflections of Sottsass' use of "simple shapes and a variety of colors." She incorporates elements of other modern designers, too, from Spanish artist-designer Jaime Hayon to the emotive work of Milanese agency Studiopepe.

Aida Muluneh

Three questions for the Ethiopian photographer.

Artworks: Aida Muluneh

Whether through cultural advocacy or ardent storytelling, Aida Muluneh's vision of the African continent is a powerful testament to the ability of photography to bridge divides. After returning to Ethiopia as an adult after living most of her life abroad, Muluneh founded the Addis Foto Fest to celebrate global exchanges made possible by photography. Such an exchange also informs her own photography practice, which has garnered critical acclaim from institutions such as African Photography Encounters in Bamako, Mali, as well as the Centre for Photographic Research and Archiving in Spilimbergo, Italy.

Body painting becomes just as much a subject in your photography as the individuals in the images. Why do you choose to work with body paint? The choice of utilizing body painting was inspired by traditional societies that adorned their bodies with body paint and also scarification. In a global context, most ancient societies' use of body decoration is closely linked with a form of expression that I find complex and quite contemporary. My goal has been to incorporate elements of the past and to present those elements within the framework of my personal expression.

I'm very curious about the Addis Foto Fest, which you founded in 2010. What was the impetus behind the festival? In my first few months back in Addis Ababa, I gave workshops at the university. I quickly realized that it wasn't just a matter of educating photographers, but also educating society on the social applications of photography. The Addis Foto Fest started as an event to bring together photographers from around the world, with the objective of connecting photographers in Africa with those beyond our borders.

You've been back in Ethiopia for about 10 years now. What has it meant to come home? The return to my birthplace has meant an adjustment to being both an insider and an outsider. Having grown up as an immigrant abroad for most of my life, I have always identified as belonging to Ethiopia, and my return came out of a need to reconnect. Returning to Ethiopia has inspired me to become the photographer I am today. Being here has taught me valuable lessons, not only about the complex dynamics unfolding within my country but also about global politics and its influences and hindrances on Ethiopia and on Africa more widely.

The 99 Series Part Two (left) and *The 99 Series Part One* (above) capture "the story we each carry, of loss, of oppressors, of victims, of disconnection," writes Muluneh.

COCLICO

COCLICO.COM

CONSCIOUSLY   ARTFULLY   ELEGANTLY

Long-distance calling: Meet the designer balancing two jobs in two countries.

Photograph: Alexander Wolfe, Location: thejamjar Dubai

JOHN CLIFFORD BURNS

Khalid Al Qasimi

Khalid Al Qasimi leads a dual career: In his hometown of Sharjah, United Arab Emirates, he is chairman of the local government's urban planning council. But when in London, he is creative director of Qasimi—a rising menswear label whose collections make baby-pink overcoats and Bedouin striped linen trousers look not only tasteful, but ready-to-wear.

You have two very different jobs. Does one ever inform the other? I studied architecture because I felt it was the pinnacle of a design education. Once you learn about structure, proportion and construction, you can view the body as a landscape.

Sharjah must be an interesting place for an urbanist. It can often be frustrating. Some of the architecture could be much better, but there's a lot of opportunity. There are also existing buildings that people just don't see. I love the modernist architecture that was built in the 1940s and 1950s— it's completely hidden. One of the projects I'm working on at the moment is a new Sharjah Architecture Triennial to reinforce the importance of these places.

Does Sharjah influence your work at Qasimi? I'm influenced by politics and society. Politics is always discussed at the dinner table in the Middle East—it's completely embedded in our culture. In the past, I felt like it was my duty to raise these issues in the West, where people often have a one-sided view of the Middle East. I was proud of that and felt that it was needed, but I don't think the industry appreciated it. Now, I take a broader approach.

Do you wear your own clothes? More and more. But it can be sad to put so much effort into them, for them only to sit in the studio for such a long time. At some point you just don't see them anymore. I do keep an archive, though.

Who brings out your best qualities? My sisters. They always call me out if need be, or else they'll champion me when I feel down or a bit unsure.

What are you like to work with? I like to take more of a democratic approach in the studio and hear everyone's opinions. I can be difficult sometimes, but it's just because I know exactly what I want.

SEAN MICHAELS

Of Buds and Birds

The sound of spring, per classical concerti.

It's easy to get springtime wrong. The history of classical music is rich with composers who seem to have never actually experienced the month of May, let alone April—composers for whom the end of winter is summed up by pretty melodies, soaring themes, bucolic strings. Basically: all lambs, no mud.

But spring is more than that. It's ice-crack and tulip bud, wet basements and birdsong, mulch and meltwater. Lambs don't just gambol: They're born too, messily. Allergies ramp up, rain clouds open, troubles surface. With the exception of Stravinsky's glorious *Rite of Spring*, teeming with primal appetites, the best-known vernal works render the season at its most banal: Schumann's exhaustingly upbeat *Spring Symphony*; Mendelssohn's dementedly Arcadian, *Looney Tunes*-like "Spring Song"; and, inescapably, the threadbare first movement of Vivaldi's *Four Seasons*.

So never mind that stuff. For me, spring is about disquiet—frozen feelings coming loose. It's the inverse of fall, where the heart is slowly stilling. In spring things dawn, break, molt, change form, grow shoots. Stravinsky's *Rite* is just an extreme portrayal—spring at its most terrifying, filled with fertile power. Rachmaninoff reflects the same vitality: His song "Spring Waters" is cheerful but riotous, a soprano running rampant over shattering piano chords. Delius captured a similar energy in

"The March of Spring," an orchestral piece from his *North Country Sketches*. Here, as with most classical music, the secret is to play it loud. Whereas modern rock and pop use sound as a fire hose, compressing as much as they can into FM radio-ready frequencies, classical music thrives on its dynamics, from whispering strings to booming horns. Listen too quietly and that power wastes away.

This isn't just true of symphonies. Solo piano works are too often relegated to background music. Compositions like Tchaikovsky's "May," from his underappreciated series *The Seasons*, thaws beautifully from cool, glacial melancholy into rushing—and nearly contented—cascades. A similar progress marks John Cage's *String Quartet in Four Parts*, from 1950. Although Cage is better known for experiments like *4'33"*, this quartet is direct and luminous, each of its movements representing a different season. The section for spring is called "Slowly Rocking" and it does just this—a back and forth of swaying phrases, alternately gorgeous and dissonant.

In truth, *this* is spring in full bloom. Seasons don't switch like records in a jukebox, the next one neatly clacking into place. They're closer to cacophonies—intermingling melodies, two songs at the same time. Spring is like summer, like autumn, like winter: It's a moment in motion, changing before you. It's always transforming; its music should too.

Sean Michaels is the author of *Us Conductors*, a novel for which he won the Scotiabank Giller Prize in 2014.

ELLIE VIOLET BRAMLEY

Word: Grit

If at first you don't succeed, dust yourself off and try again.

Etymology: From the Old English word *grēot* meaning dust, earth or gravel. *Meaning:* To have grit means to have courage and resolve, strength of character, pluck, mettle. It's a word that feels onomatopoeic: It embodies itself, roundly and confidently; say it out loud and you will feel grittier.

But drill down and grit means slightly different things depending on whom you're talking to. To Angela Duckworth, a psychologist and a professor at the University of Pennsylvania, whose work has brought grit into focus in the past few years, it means a passion and perseverance for long-term goals. Grit, she writes, "is about having what some researchers call an 'ultimate concern'—a goal you care about so much that it organizes and gives meaning to almost everything you do." And it is holding steadfast to that goal, "even when you fall down, mess up, or when progress is faltering." In

Duckworth's school of thought, it has to do with stamina—treating life as a marathon rather than a sprint. For other researchers, such as Gale Lucas of the USC Institute for Creative Technologies, grit is about the sprints, too. A marathon is made up of a series of legs, after all. "It's the courage people have to push through the fear of failure and to persist in the face of potential failure."

So, can we cultivate grit and learn to persevere despite setbacks? In short, yes. Mindset is key. By cultivating what Stanford psychology professor Carol Dweck calls the "growth mindset"—an understanding that our brains can grow when challenged—we are less likely to stagnate and settle for less. She cites a school in Chicago where, if students didn't pass one of their courses they were given a grade of "Not Yet," which makes you understand, she explains, "that you're on a learning curve.

It gives you a path into the future." Rather than writing ourselves off at the first sign of failure, we should trust that we can learn and improve; this is the power of "yet."

But there can be limits to the benefits of the kind of doggedness that gritty individuals often display—it can, says Gale Lucas, be a "double-edged sword." For often the gritty individual is an optimistic one, too. And while a rosy outlook is in general no bad thing, people can lose sight of what it's worth being gritty for—as well as what goals are realistic for them personally. Those people, Lucas says, "might not know when to quit."

To learn what's worth pursuing, then, gritty individuals "should try to get more objective indicators… Seek the advice of friends, family and counselors," guides Lucas. And "try to figure out how likely it is that you're going to succeed. Is it time to cut your losses?" In other words, use your grit responsibly.

Photograph: Imagno/Getty Images

TOUCH WOOD

by Ellie Violet Bramley

These elegant wooden pieces speak to the ability of craft to marry beauty and strength. Whether it's a one-of-a-kind biomorphic wooden sculpture or a hand-carved solid wood centerpiece made from the trunks of walnut, cherry, maple and oak trees, wood as design makes for a valuable lesson in what can be achieved with time and calm. As transcendentalist poet Ralph Waldo Emerson would have it, nature's secret is patience. Top: Finn Juhl Handmade Wooden Bowl. Middle: Biomorphic Carved Wood Bowl from The Line. Bottom: Large Wooden Abstract Sculpture from The Line.

In Praise of Butter

Spreading some love for saturated fat.

Elaine Khosrova never intended to write an entire book on butter. A former pastry chef and food writer, her first exposure to butter's wide-ranging properties came when she was assigned to a butter tasting. "I hadn't expected to experience such a range of color, flavor and texture among the 12 or so samples," she recalls. "Knowing butter is essentially made from a simple process of agitation using just one ingredient—cream—I couldn't account for why there was such variation."

Khosrova already had a soft spot for dairy; she'd founded a specialty cheese magazine in 2008. But butter was unplumbed terrain for her, and as she began to delve deeper, she realized that its cultural legacy had been overlooked in culinary literature, too. She began work on *Butter: A Rich History*, an ode to butter's enduring role in civilization. From the Vedic Aryans of India, who "sprinkled melted butter on the flames of a bonfire to make them leap and crackle" as they worshipped their fire god, to ancient Ireland, where Druids "buried butter in the bog as an offering to the fairies," butter has enjoyed a revered role in society for millennia.

Only the Romans were disdainful, believing it to be the food of barbarians. As butter lost its religious symbolism, it assumed economic clout. Internationally traded by the Irish, Dutch and the Danish, the creamy fat also became an integral component in French and American cuisine. But by the 1960s, butter's fortunes waned as scientists and governmental agencies vilified animal fats in a misguided effort to combat heart disease. Only now is it beginning to reemerge from beneath this cloud of stigma, helped in part by a backlash against margarine, its chief competitor. As Khosrova notes, "the epidemic of obesity and diabetes has many people questioning the low-fat, no-fat advice they've been given for decades."

With butter fashionable again, aspiring connoisseurs have an abundance of varieties to choose from. Khosrova recommends sampling different brands side by side to appreciate their subtle differences; she also suggests investing in pricier grass-fed butters. Tempted to slather it on a baguette for your taste test? Resist the urge: You'll be surprised at the flavors you uncover when you try butter on its own.

On the uneasy dance between knowledge and information.

British-Bangladeshi choreographer and performer Akram Khan challenges the seeming contradiction between static sculptures and moving dancers. The power of the statue, he says, lies in how its immobility prompts movement in the observer while, conversely, the moving body can make the viewer still. He's been exploring this theme since he began creating his unique fusion of contemporary and South Asian classical dance traditions in 2000. Speaking from London, where he co-founded the Akram Khan Company, he addresses our tendency today to privilege information over wisdom, the connection between dance and our ancient past and the invaluable reactions of children.

Your 2010 work, *Vertical Road*, which was inspired by traditions in Sufi Islam and the poetry of Rumi, meditates on the difficulties of wresting oneself from the horizontal road of earthly time and living along the emotional, transcendent "vertical" path. Has that latter road become even harder to follow of late? Our ancient myths were based on gods. Now we've replaced gods with humans because we're able to create technology and use it to our advantage. But I think that technology will replace us when it figures out that it doesn't need us any longer, and then it will be the new god.

In filming a new documentary, *Can We Live with Robots?*, for the UK's Channel 4, I've asked people who work in that field: What makes us human? I think we need to return to this question because we're so numb today, which is probably why we're unhappy. It's a very traumatic time, but we're not feeling it. We're living in a moment when governments employ shock treatments at an epic scale, and people are occupied and made numb while massive changes occur. We're unable to move forward or backward in any way.

What are the benefits of change and transformation? All change is violence because we are very accustomed to habit. When you create a ritual by doing something again and again, it—and you— slowly become absent, because it's familiar. You move away from the present, where you should be living. We must continue evolving. This isn't about changing govern-

CHARLES SHAFAIEH

Akram Khan

Akram, 43, will retire from full-length performances in 2018. His last solo will be in *Xenos*—a new production to mark the centenary of the First World War.

"Dance carries our ancestors inside us like a living museum that's constantly transforming."

ments; that's not enough. Every individual must transform in order to survive, and this is violent because anything uncomfortable is violent to your senses. And you never know what you're going to change into. Even when you plan it, it's unknown.

Have we entered an age of anesthetization, in which feelings of discomfort, whether through art or other means, are vilified as we search for constant comfort and happiness? I think so. The capitalist system isn't working. We have grown up watching advertisements that tell us that we need this or that, and our hunger and thirst for more new things has not dwindled. It's actually growing, even after we meet our basic needs of safety, shelter, food and water. We think we require much more to be happy, but we're not happy with the hundreds of thousands of things that we buy every day.

The thing is, the old capitalist and imperialist myths have not quite died, and the new myths haven't yet been born. We're in a myth gap. And the problem with creating new myths is that, every year, we have to create more new myths. We can't keep up, especially with the speed of technology and its advancements.

How can art, and dance in particular, speak to this present crisis? Art is the bedrock of what makes us human. Our sense of reflection, of learning, happens through seeing and exploring the world and our stories through mediums other than politics and television. It allows us to see those stories in a more ancient way. The popular conception is that with each generation, we become more intelligent. Many ancient tribes, however, believe that with each generation we become less wise. We feel we're more intelligent because of our immense access to information, but that's not the same as knowledge. Knowledge is information that is fully embodied and experienced. There's a huge difference between the two, and right now, we are in awe of information rather than wisdom. Dance carries our ancestors inside us like a living museum that's constantly transforming. But dance is simultaneously carrying with it the future. The body is a means to explore and express how we're feeling in a very sacred, spiritual way. It allows us to be in touch with our five senses again, to take us out of numbness. The body doesn't lie. Especially on stage. When you see people lie in dance, you know it's a lie.

What can we learn from children, in terms of experiencing art and gaining wisdom? Children constantly remind me that everything is possible. They're very connected to the truth. When something isn't working, they switch off, and when it's genuine, they click in. We've learned the art of hiding what we feel, but children don't do that. They haven't yet conformed to numbness. We educate them into that, but in their youth, they are purely listening to their instincts—which is how we all used to be. At the heart of creativity lies instinct, and at the heart of instinct lies creativity.

43 — 112

Features

Goodbye to All That

How many miles to Babylon?
Three score miles and ten—
Can I get there by candlelight?
Yes, and back again—
If your feet are nimble and light
You can get there by candlelight.

It is easy to see the beginnings of things, and harder to see the ends. I can remember now, with a clarity that makes the nerves in the back of my neck constrict, when New York began for me, but I cannot lay my finger upon the moment it ended, can never cut through the ambiguities and second starts and broken resolves to the exact place on the page where the heroine is no longer as optimistic as she once was. When I first saw New York I was twenty, and it was summertime, and I got off a DC-7 at the old Idlewild temporary terminal in a new dress which had seemed very smart in Sacramento but seemed less smart already, even in the old Idlewild temporary terminal, and the warm air smelled of mildew and some instinct, programmed by all the movies I had ever seen and all the songs I had ever read about New York, informed me that it would never be quite the same again. In fact it never was. Some time later there was a song in the jukeboxes on the Upper East Side that went "but where is the schoolgirl who used to be me," and if it was late enough at night I used to wonder that. I know now that almost everyone wonders something like that, sooner or later and no matter what he or she is doing, but one of the mixed blessings of being twenty and twenty-one and even twenty-three is the conviction that nothing like this, all evidence to the contrary notwithstanding, has ever happened to anyone before.

Of course it might have been some other city, had circumstances been different and the time been different and had I been different, might have been Paris or Chicago or even San Francisco, but because I am talking about myself I am talking here about New York. That first night I opened my window on the bus into town and watched for the skyline, but all I could see were the wastes of Queens and big signs that said MIDTOWN TUNNEL THIS LANE and then a flood of summer rain (even that seemed remarkable and exotic, for I had come out of the West where there was no summer rain), and for the next three days I sat wrapped in blankets in a hotel room air conditioned to 35 degrees and tried to get over a cold and a high fever. It did not occur to me to call a doctor, because I knew none, and although it did occur to me to call the desk and ask that the air conditioner be turned off, I never called, because I did not know how much to tip whoever might come—was anyone ever so young? I am here to tell you that someone was. All I could do during those years was talk long-distance to the boy I already knew I would never marry in the spring. I would stay in New York, I told him, just six months, and I could see the Brooklyn Bridge from my window. As it turned out the bridge was the Triborough, and I stayed eight years.

In retrospect it seems to me that those days before I knew the names of all the bridges were happier than the ones that came later, but perhaps you will see that as we go along. Part of what I want to tell you is what it is like to be young in New York, how six months can become eight years with the deceptive ease of a film dissolve, for that is how those years appear to me now, in a long sequence of sentimental dissolves and old-fashioned trick shots—the Seagram Building fountains dissolve into snowflakes, I enter a revolving door at twenty and come out a good deal older, and on a dif-

ferent street. But most particularly I want to explain to you, and in the process perhaps to myself, why I no longer live in New York. It is often said that New York is a city for only the very rich and the very poor. It is less often said that New York is also, at least for those of us who came there from somewhere else, a city only for the very young.

I remember once, one cold bright December evening in New York, suggesting a friend who complained of having been around too long that he come with me to a party where there would be, I assured him with the bright resourcefulness of twenty-three, "new faces." He laughed literally until he choked, and I had to roll down the taxi window and hit him on the back. "New faces," he said finally, "don't tell me about new faces." It seemed that the last time he had gone to a party where he had been promised "new faces," there had been fifteen people in the room, and he had already slept with five of the women and owed money to all but two of the men. I laughed with him, but the first snow had just begun to fall and the big Christmas trees glittered yellow and white as far as I could see up Park Avenue and I had a new dress and it would be a long while before I would come to understand the particular moral of the story.

It would be a long while because, quite simply, I was in love with New York. I do not mean "love" in any colloquial way, I mean that I was in love with the city, the way you love the first person who ever touches you and you never love anyone quite that way again. I remember walking across Sixty-second Street one twilight that first spring, or the second spring, they were all alike for a while. I was late to meet someone but I stopped at Lexington Avenue and bought a peach and stood on the corner eat-

"Was anyone ever so young?" asks Joan Didion in "Goodbye to All That"—the essay in which the seminal writer reflects on how six months in New York turned into eight years, and how her youth slipped out of view. It was an essay that spawned a genre—the writer who falls in and out of love with a city and leaves it behind—but Didion's remains inimitable, as alive and relevant today as when it was first published in 1967.

ing it and knew that I had come out of the West and reached the mirage. I could taste the peach and feel the soft air blowing from a subway grating on my legs and I could smell lilac and garbage and expensive perfume and I knew that it would cost something sooner or later—because I did not belong there, did not come from there—but when you are twenty-two or twenty-three, you figure that later you will have a high emotional balance, and be able to pay whatever it costs. I still believed in possibilities then, still had the sense, so peculiar to New York, that something extraordinary would happen any minute, any day, any month. I was making only $65 or $70 a week then ("Put yourself in Hattie Carnegie's hands," I was advised without the slightest trace of irony by an editor of the magazine for which I worked), so little money that some weeks I had to charge food at Bloomingdale's gourmet shop in order to eat, a fact which went unmentioned in the letters I wrote to California. I never told my father that I needed money because then he would have sent it, and I would never know if I could do it by myself. At that time making a living seemed a game to me, with arbitrary but quite inflexible rules. And except on a certain kind of winter evening—six-thirty in the Seventies, say, already dark and bitter with a wind off the river, when I would be walking very fast toward a bus and would look in the bright windows of brownstones and see cooks working in clean kitchens and imagine women lighting candles on the floor above and beautiful children being bathed on the floor above that—except on nights like those, I never felt poor; I had the feeling that if I needed money I could always get it. I could write a syndicated column for teenagers under the name "Debbi Lynn" or I could smuggle gold into India or I

could become a $100 call girl, and none of it would matter.

Nothing was irrevocable; everything was within reach. Just around every corner lay something curious and interesting, something I had never before seen or done or known about. I could go to a party and meet someone who called himself Mr. Emotional Appeal and ran The Emotional Appeal Institute or Tina Onassis Blandford or a Florida cracker who was then a regular on what he called "the Big C," the Southampton-El Morocco circuit ("I'm well connected on the Big C, honey," he would tell me over collard greens on his vast borrowed terrace), or the widow of the celery king of the Harlem market or a piano salesman from Bonne Terre, Missouri, or someone who had already made and lost two fortunes in Midland, Texas. I could make promises to myself and to other people and there would be all the time in the world to keep them. I could stay up all night and make mistakes, and none of them would count.

You see I was in a curious position in New York: it never occurred to me that I was living a real life there. In my imagination I was always there for just another few months, just until Christmas or Easter or the first warm day in May. For that reason I was most comfortable with the company of Southerners. They seemed to be in New York as I was, on some indefinitely extended leave from wherever they belonged, disciplined to consider the future, temporary exiles who always knew when the flights left for New Orleans or Memphis or Richmond or, in my case, California. Someone who lives with a plane schedule in the drawer lives on a slightly different calendar. Christmas, for example, was a difficult season. Other people could take it in stride, going to Stowe or going abroad or

going for the day to their mothers' places in Connecticut; those of us who believed that we lived somewhere else would spend it making and canceling airline reservations, waiting for weatherbound flights as if for the last plane out of Lisbon in 1940, and finally comforting one another, those of us who were left, with oranges and mementos and smoked-oyster stuffings of childhood, gathering close, colonials in a far country.

Which is precisely what we were. I am not sure that it is possible for anyone brought up in the East to appreciate entirely what New York, the idea of New York, means to those of us who came out of the West and the South. To an Eastern child, particularly a child who has always had an uncle on Wall Street and who has spent several hundred Saturdays first at F.A.O. Schwarz and being fitted for shoes at Best's and then waiting under the Biltmore clock and dancing to Lester Lanin, New York is just a city, albeit *the* city, a plausible place for people to live. But to those of us who came from places where no one had heard of Lester Lanin and Grand Central Station was a Saturday radio program, where Wall Street and Fifth Avenue and Madison Avenue were not places at all but abstractions ("Money," and "High Fashion," and "The Hucksters"), New York was no mere city. It was instead an infinitely romantic notion, the mysterious nexus of all love and money and power, the shining and perishable dream itself. To think of "living" there was to reduce the miraculous to the mundane; one does not "live" at Xanadu.

In fact it was difficult in the extreme for me to understand those young women for whom New York was not simply an ephemeral Estoril but a real place, girls who bought toasters and installed new cabinets in their apartments and committed themselves to some reasonable future. I never bought any furniture in New York. For a year or so I lived in other people's apartments; after that I lived in the Nineties in an apartment furnished entirely with things taken from storage by a friend whose wife had moved away. And when I left the apartment in the Nineties (that was when I was leaving everything, when it was all breaking up) I left everything in it, even my winter clothes and the map of Sacramento County I had hung on the bedroom wall to remind me who I was, and I moved into a monastic four-room floor-through on Seventy-fifth Street. "Monastic" is perhaps misleading here, implying some chic severity; until after I was married and my husband moved some furniture in, there was nothing at all in those four rooms except a cheap double mattress and box springs, ordered by telephone the day I decided to move, and two French garden chairs lent me by a friend who imported them. (It strikes me now that the people I knew in New York all had curious and self-defeating sidelines. They imported garden chairs which did not sell very well at Hammacher Schlemmer or they tried to market hair staighteners in Harlem or they ghosted exposés of Murder Incorporated for Sunday supplements. I think that perhaps none of us was very serious, *engagé* only about our most private lives.)

All I ever did to that apartment was hang fifty yards of yellow theatrical silk across the bedroom windows, because I had some idea that the gold light would make me feel better, but I did not bother to weight the curtains correctly and all that summer the long panels of transparent golden silk would blow out the windows and get tangled and drenched in afternoon thunderstorms. That was the year, my twenty-eighth, when I was discovering that not all of the promises would be kept, that some things are in fact irrevocable and that it had counted after all, every evasion and every procrastination, every word, all of it.

That is what it was all about, wasn't it? Promises? Now when New York comes back to me it comes in hallucinatory flashes, so clinically detailed that I sometimes wish that memory would effect the distortion with which it is commonly credited. For a lot of the time I was in New York I used a perfume called *Fleurs de Rocaille*, and then *L'Air du Temps*, and now the slightest trace of either can short-circuit my connections for the rest of the day. Nor can I smell Henri Bendel jasmine soap without falling back into the past, or the particular mixture of spices used for boiling crabs. There were barrels of crab boil in a Czech place in the Eighties where I once shopped. Smells, of course, are notorious memory stimuli, but there are other things which affect me the same way. Blue-and-white striped sheets. Vermouth cassis. Some faded nightgowns which were new in 1959 or 1960, and some chiffon scarves I bought about the same time.

I suppose that a lot of us who have been very young in New York have the same scenes in our home screens. I remember sitting in a lot of apartments with a slight headache about five o'clock in the morning. I had a friend who could not sleep, and he knew a few other people who had the same trouble, and we would watch the sky lighten and have a last drink with no ice and then go home in the early morning, when the streets were clean and wet (had it rained in the night? we never knew) and the few cruising taxis still had their headlights on and the only color was the red and green of traffic signals. The White Rose bars opened very early in the morning; I recall waiting in one of them to watch an astronaut go into space, waiting so long that at the moment it actually happened I had my eyes not on the television screen but on a cockroach on the tile floor. I liked the bleak branches above Washington Square at dawn, and the monochromatic flatness of Second Avenue, the fire escapes and the grilled storefronts peculiar and empty in their perspective.

It is relatively hard to fight at six-thirty or seven in the morning, without any sleep, which was perhaps one reason why we stayed up all night, and it seemed to me a pleasant time of day. The windows were shuttered in that apartment in the Nineties and I could sleep for a few hours and then go to work. I could work then on two or three hours' sleep and a container of coffee from Chock Full O' Nuts. I liked going to work, liked the soothing and satisfactory rhythm of getting out a magazine, liked the orderly progression of four-color closings and two-color closings and black-and-white closings and then The Product, no abstraction but something which looked effortlessly glossy and could be picked up on a newsstand and weighed in the hand. I liked all the minutiae of proofs and layouts, liked working late on the nights the magazine went to press, sitting and reading *Variety* and waiting for the copy desk to call. From my office, I could look across town to the weather signal on the Mutual of New York Building and the lights that alternately spelled out TIME and LIFE above Rockefeller Plaza; that pleased me obscurely, and so did walking uptown in the mauve eight o'clocks of early summer evenings and looking at things, Lowestoft tureens in Fifty-seventh Street windows, people in evening clothes trying to get taxis, the trees just coming into full leaf, the lambent air, all the sweet promises of money and summer. Some years passed, but I

> "The last time he had gone to a party where he had been promised 'new faces,' there had been fifteen people in the room, and he had already slept with five of the women and owed money to all but two of the men."

still did not lose that sense of wonder about New York. I began to cherish the loneliness of it, the sense that at any given time no one need know where I was or what I was doing. I liked walking, from the East River over to the Hudson and back on brisk days, down around the Village on warm days. A friend would leave me the key to her apartment in the West Village when she was out of town, and sometimes I would just move down there, because by that time the telephone was beginning to bother me (the canker, you see, was already in the rose) and not many people had that number. I remember one day when someone who did have the West Village number came to pick me up for lunch there, and we both had hangovers, and I cut my finger opening him a beer and burst into tears, and we walked to a Spanish restaurant and drank Bloody Marys and *gazpacho* until we felt better. I was not then guilt-ridden about spending afternoons that way, because I still had all the afternoons in the world.

And even that late in the game I still liked going to parties, all parties, bad parties, Saturday-afternoon parties given by recently married couples who lived in Stuyvesant Town, West Side parties given by unpublished or failed writers who served cheap red wine and talked about going to Guadalajara, Village parties where all the guests worked for advertising agencies and voted for Reform Democrats, press parties at Sardi's, the worst kind of parties. You will have perceived by now that I was not one to profit by the experience of others, that it was a very long time indeed before I stopped believing in new faces and began to understand the lesson in that story, which was that it is distinctly possible to stay too long at the Fair.

I could not tell you when I began to understand that. All I know is that it was very bad

when I was twenty-eight. Everything that was said to me I seemed to have heard before, and I could no longer listen. I could no longer sit in little bars near Grand Central and listen to someone complaining of his wife's inability to cope with the help while he missed another train to Connecticut. I no longer had any interest in hearing about the advances other people had received from their publishers, about plays which were having second-act trouble in Philadelphia, or about people I would like very much if only I would come out and meet them. I had already met them, always. There were certain parts of the city which I had to avoid. I could not bear upper Madison Avenue on weekday mornings (this was a particularly inconvenient aversion, since I then lived just fifty or sixty feet east of Madison), because I would see women walking Yorkshire terriers and shopping at Gristede's, and some Veblenesque gorge would rise in my throat. I could not go to Times Square in the afternoon, or to the New York Public Library for any reason whatsoever. One day I could not go into a Schrafft's; the next it would be Bonwit Teller.

I hurt the people I cared about, and insulted those I did not. I cut myself off from the one person who was closer to me than any other. I cried until I was not even aware when I was crying and when I was not, cried in elevators and in taxis and in Chinese laundries, and when I went to the doctor, he said only that I seemed to be depressed, and that I should see a "specialist." He wrote down a psychiatrist's name and address for me, but I did not go.

Instead I got married, which as it turned out was a very good thing to do but badly timed, since I still could not walk on upper Madison Avenue in the mornings and still could not talk to people and still cried in Chinese laun-

dries. I had never before understood what "despair" meant, and I am not sure that I understand now, but I understood that year. Of course I could not work. I could not even get dinner with any degree of certainty, and I would sit in the apartment on Seventy-fifth Street paralyzed until my husband would call from his office and say gently that I did not have to get dinner, that I could meet him at Michael's Pub or at Toots Shor's or at Sardi's East. And then one morning in April (we had been married in January) he called and told me that he wanted to get out of New York for a while, that he would take a six-month leave of absence, that we would go somewhere.

It was three years ago he told me that, and we have lived in Los Angeles since. Many of the people we knew in New York think this a curious aberration, and in fact tell us so. There is no possible, no adequate answer to that, and so we give certain stock answers, the answers everyone gives. I talk about how difficult it would be for us to "afford" to live in New York right now, about how much "space" we need. All I mean is that I was very young in New York, and that at some point the golden rhythm was broken, and I am not that young anymore. The last time I was in New York was in a cold January, and everyone was ill and tired. Many of the people I used to know there had moved to Dallas or had gone on Antabuse or had bought a farm in New Hampshire. We stayed ten days, and then we took an afternoon flight back to Los Angeles, and on the way home from the airport that night I could see the moon on the Pacific and smell jasmine all around and we both knew that there was no longer any point in keeping the apartment we still kept in New York. There were years when I called Los Angeles "the Coast," but they seem a long time ago.

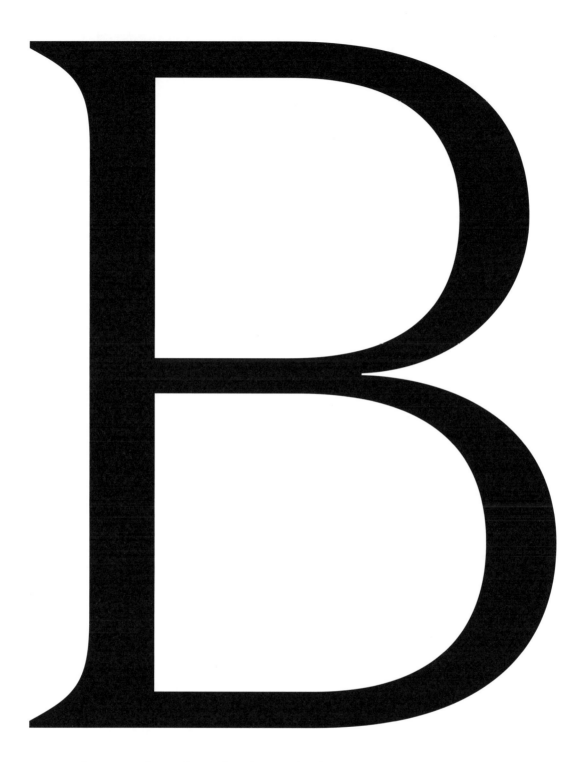

enjamin Clementine dropped out of nowhere. Before his ascension as a musician and poet, he was drifting around Paris with no money, no connections and not much to fall back on but a keyboard, his creativity and a charisma that belied his years and circumstances. In the years since, following the release of two acclaimed albums, The New York Times saw fit to deem Clementine a "creative genius," the British press as one of the most influential people in the UK. As with most legendary tales, Clementine's is a story often told. In fact, he's somewhat bored of it himself. A born raconteur, however, Clementine is writing a captivating next chapter.

Words by Priscilla Ward & Photography by Katie McCurdy

Benjamin Clementine is a lesson in dichotomies: The 28-year-old pianist and songwriter exudes the wisdom of someone twice his age while questioning everything about the world around him with the vulnerability and naivety of a child. His songwriting is intensely personal, often dealing with themes of solitude and survival, and yet the artist himself is protective of the narrative surrounding his rise to fame. His story—of homelessness in Paris, attempted suicide, rags-to-riches discovery and success—is overly simplistic, he says. The truth is much murkier and more nuanced, as real-life stories so often are.

The youngest of five children, Clementine was raised by his grandmother in a middle-class household in Edmonton, London. She died when he was 11 years old, after which he was obliged to move in with his parents, who divorced when he was 16. At 19, he left London for Paris, where he began writing music and eking out a living busking in metro stations. We meet in Los Angeles as Clementine prepares to depart on a tour to promote his latest album, *I Tell a Fly*, a follow-up to his critically acclaimed debut, *At Least for Now*, which earned him the Mercury Music Prize in 2015. Wearing a suit with fur-lined Gucci mules, his Afro mimicking an intricately designed gentlemen's hat, Clementine recounts his emotional inheritance and describes how, despite his worldwide acclaim, he still does not consider himself a singer.

You spent some time living in New York recently. What was your impression? There were a lot of people and it was noisy. All the shops were trendy and the restaurants were expensive. Everyone was dressed fashionably. It was like Europe, and that's not the America that I read about when I was a kid. That America was Albuquerque, Arizona and Texas.

Your song "Jupiter" feels like an immigrant's tale. Is it based on personal experience? Americans like the word *alien*. I was called an "alien of extraordinary ability" on my visa and that was the first thing that made me go, "Wow. What the hell? An alien of extraordinary abilities? Okay, well I'm going to start making music. So be it, I'm going to be the alien."

Right: Clementine wears a sweater by Dries Van Noten, T-shirt by COS and trousers by The Kooples. Below: He wears a jacket by A.P.C. and sweater by COS.

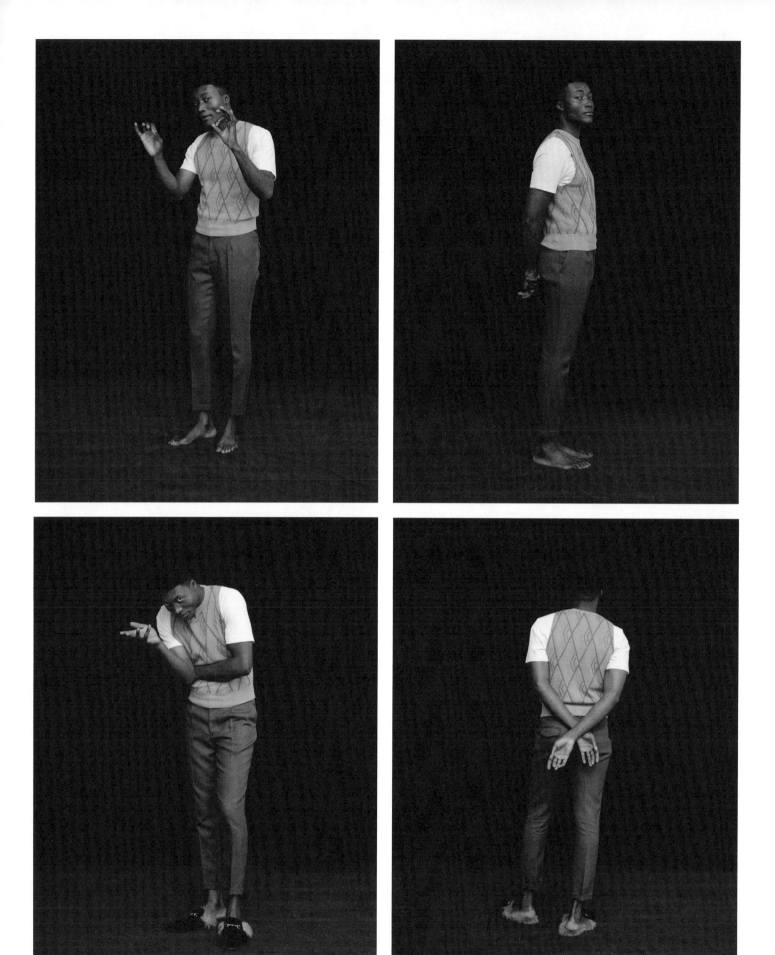

Clementine wears a sweater by Dries Van Noten, T-shirt by COS, trousers by The Kooples and his own Gucci shoes.

Your family is originally from Ghana? Well, that's what they say.

What do you mean by that? It's hard to talk about a country that I've never been to or had any affiliations with. My parents were immigrants who came to England. I'm not interested—it's my father's stuff. I was born in England. And if I can't even build a relationship with my father, then why would I concern myself with where he came from? It's a very complicated issue.

What's your relationship like with your mother? It's almost the same. I grew up with my grandmother and she was very young when she died. I only spent five years with my parents, between the ages of 11 and 16 before they divorced and left. I had to work for myself and find the meaning of life.

Do you think your early self-reliance has affected your work? People are always going to come against your ambitions, your dreams and what you want. We're all human beings—that should be no surprise. But there's beauty in everything. I think you should just go wherever you want to go. And if you want to stay, then stay. There's always going to be someone who isn't going to agree with what you think or what you believe in.

And where is it that you want to go next? I'm thinking about going to live in Albuquerque, New Mexico. When I moved to Paris, it was because I just felt that I had to go. I didn't have money, but I found a way. I felt that I had something to do there. The reason I went to New York was that I felt I wanted to go to New York. I guess Albuquerque just feels like the next place. I would like to go there to possibly write.

Can you tell me a little bit about where you were in life when you wrote the song "Condolence"? I wrote that song when I had tried to commit suicide for the second time in Paris. Surviving those suicidal tendencies made me write that song. "If you cut yourself or if you jump off the bridge, would anyone care? Would anyone know?" I had realized that going away wouldn't really make any difference to anyone. When I was in that process, I wrote a bunch of songs.

What was your life like in Paris? In Paris, I was just a ghost. Right now, I'm paying taxes. I've got a house. I've got my name on it. But back then, no one knew who I was. I was a phantom. I was just trolling around the streets, talking to people.

Since then, you've performed around the world. How did you make it to Carnegie Hall? I believe that if you ask for money, you'll only live for a day. I realized that I had to befriend people. Eventually, I started going to people's birthday parties or they'd invite me to dinner. Friendship was the key to surviving. I could certainly compare that time in my life to the American dream—survival of the fittest.

What does the American dream mean to you now? Americans are free. Bringing that to what I went through a couple of years back, all I wanted to do was live and become myself. That was the dream for me—moving away to find your ground and be who you want to be. Believing in what you want, whether it's a religion or a philosophy, being spiritual or living healthy, or just finding someone that you could love and cherish and care for. So, I guess now I'm doing whatever the so-called American dream is.

Your music has a deeply spiritual undertone to it. What role does religion play in your own life? I'm from a Roman Catholic family. My grandmother was very strict and so we went to church almost every day. I know that it's such a powerful ingredient. I've taken principles that I've learned from the Bible, but I sincerely and graciously believe in love. After all of my traveling, my doubts and my battles, I just realized that all I wanted to do was to be loved and to love. That's all I wanted. Of course, there will be money here and there. There will be attention. But truthfully, all I wanted was to be loved because possibly I wasn't when I was a kid. So, I was searching for that. That's what I think it's all about.

"All I wanted to do was live and become myself. That was the dream for me."

Clementine wears a sweater by
A.P.C. and trousers by COS.

"I have things that I want to say, and this is the way that I want to say it."

Above: Clementine wears a jacket and trousers by A.P.C. and a sweater by COS. Left: He wears his own MM6 Maison Margiela suit.

Your music doesn't fit into any particular genre. It doesn't follow a model for what's right and what's wrong, and there's no following of a particular beat or rhythm. How would you describe it? What comes first is what I want to express. Earlier on in this conversation, we spoke about my father. After my grandmother died, there wasn't a father figure in my life, or I didn't really respect him. I never had that someone telling me to "Do this, do that." Having had that experience, I find it very hard to listen to what someone—like my record label—has got to say about my music. I've followed my instincts and my intuition so much that I'm used to it now. That's why my music sounds the way that it sounds. I have things that I want to say, and this is the way that I want to say it.

What sort of music did you listen to while growing up? I listened to classical music when I was a kid because my parents didn't want me to listen to pop music. I could get away with classical music because there were no words. I like when music comes to me. I don't like searching for it and searching for it. It's like meeting somebody that you've fallen in love with. You don't go around choosing their name. That's how I see music.

I read that you learned to use your voice while busking. I still don't believe that I'm a singer. Real singers for me are opera singers or contemporary singers like Beyoncé and Rihanna and all of those guys. I think I'm more of a speaker. I speak my mind, I speak what I write, and I try to find a sound that somehow accompanies it.

Your approach to performance is theatrical. How do you come up with these pieces? On my second album, I wanted to talk about matters of *now*—matters that concern me. I remember waking up in New York and seeing Clinton and Trump debating on a stage—like theater. I realized that if I'm going to talk about these sorts of things which are very, very important—you know, really impactful—I must make it really theatrical and make it more like a story so that people can just take it to wherever they want to take it. Music is all about play.

Where do you find your sartorial inspiration? It's a bit like how I make my music. There are no rules. If it fits and I like it, I'll just put it on whether it's female or male. The first coat that I ever wore was from a rubbish bin in Paris. I wore it for about a year and a half. It looked horrible and was really dirty, but I didn't care. If I didn't have that coat, I would have gotten really cold. And the coat affected me somehow—the way I moved and the way I walked. It made me feel protected, like no one was going to hurt me. I think I've kept that. When I wear something, I want to feel protected.

What do you do for fun when you aren't working on your music? I like to walk because it's refreshing and makes you think. Most of my songs were made out of walking.

What's your favorite meal? I like Italian food, and I can't help but like New York steak and eggs. I had that yesterday morning.

Do you cook Italian food yourself? Yeah, I do. I like me some linguine.

I know you have to leave soon. Where are you headed to? I'm headed back to London, but I'm moving over here as soon as possible. At the very beginning of this conversation, you asked me where I'm from. It's so confusing. Most of the time I'll just say, "I'm from England." But after being called an alien, I think that's pretty much what I am. I could say I'm English-African or Franco-Anglo-African and all of that nonsense. In the simplest terms, I could quite possibly call myself an alien. I'm an alien, or so the American man thinks.

Clementine wears a coat and shirt by COS. Overleaf left: He wears a suit by Hermès and a top by COS.

Right: He wears his own MM6 Maison Margiela suit and Gucci shoes.

FEATURES

Words by *David Plaisant* & Photography by *Greg Cox*

At Home With:
Emmanuel De Bayser

On the Right Bank, a design store owner moves into a new pied-à-terre.

One could say that the area around Parc Monceau in Paris'
8th Arrondissement is swanky, but that would rather miss
the point: The neighborhood is quintessentially Parisian.
The park itself is a delightful oasis of 19th-century splen-
dor and the surrounding streets and boulevards have a se-
renely moneyed air. It is here that affable Parisian Emmanuel De Bayser has just completed renovations on a spacious, light-filled apartment.
He makes an animated host. "I've been working on this apartment for a
long time," he says of his new place—a labor of love that included a to-
tal refit, decoration and, crucially for an interiors collector, furnishing.
"Perhaps as long as six months," he figures. It's hardly an epoch, but De
Bayser is clearly someone who doesn't wait around.

The project played second fiddle to his day job running The Corner
Berlin—the successful concept store he cofounded some 1,000 kilome-
ters away in the German capital. There, on Mitte's Gendarmenmarkt, he
has also created another intimate apartment to house both himself and
some extraordinary design pieces. The modern, mainly mid-century
refinement of his Berlin home is something that De Bayser has always
wanted to create in Paris—something he is hoping his new apartment
(much larger than his former abode) will help him achieve.

"It was a little bit too small to allow the pieces to breathe," he says of
his previous address (shown throughout). Did he choose the new apartment with his furniture collection in mind, then? "Yes definitely," De
Bayser confirms. "Once you have that in mind, you really want to get
on—to fill the place and finish it." There is nothing slapdash or facile in
his approach to creating a home, however. Influences on De Bayser's taste
hark back to 19th-century decorative arts and architecture as much as
they celebrate sweeping modernist curves and angles. He corrects himself: "Well, in fact I'm never finished! The apartments always evolve."

There is a charming dichotomy between many aspects of De Bayser's life and personality: between the fast-paced and considered, the

"Paris means all the tradition and culture, and Berlin means being more adventurous."

Left: A trio of vases by Georges
Jouve complement *Flächenraum
612*, a painting by German
artist Bernd Berner.

Styling: Sven Alberding

"I'm never finished! The apartments always evolve."

classically inspired and modernist-minded, between work and home in two of Europe's great (and radically different) cities. All of this is something that informs De Bayser's taste and approach to interior design. His collection of furniture may be varied, but it shows a definite francophone flavor.

"I started to collect my first objects from the 1950s when I was maybe 22," he says of a lifelong passion for an era evident in all of his apartments. A striking arrangement of Pierre Jeanneret armchairs and couch dominates the main living room, for example. The set, with its distinctive V-leg formation, was designed by Jeanneret for Le Corbusier's modernist vision for the urban plans and architecture of Chandigarh, India. Made of matured teak and upholstered with hide, De Bayser's pieces are angular, soft and kept impossibly white. This cluster of chairs surrounds a reflective Ron Arad coffee table from the 1990s. Next door, a dining room is arranged with a playful menagerie of Jean Prouvé chairs. To punctuate the furniture—or almost as if to offer footprints—De Bayser has used ceramic pieces by the likes of Georges Jouve, mostly in a deep ink-black hue.

Though drawn to modernist postwar pieces, De Bayser is also influenced by the 19th-century, mainly Haussmannian architecture in the surrounding Parc Monceau area. There is something old-fashioned about De Bayser, who, with both parents and grandparents claiming the city as home, is born-and-bred Parisian. He laughs this off immediately and refutes the suggestion that he is counter-contemporary in any way. "There were artists and art dealers in my family, so I was surrounded by aesthetics—paintings, furniture, objects." But it's easy to see how this cultural training has influenced him through osmosis: "I distinctly remember being a child and hearing constant conversations about these objects, and also how each one had a story," he adds.

Despite De Bayser's penchant for what he calls "classic Parisian chic," there isn't the slightest bit of stuffiness about him. On the contrary, he is exuberant and fun-loving—especially when talking about his interiors. He is also very keen to shirk any hint of elitism: "For me, it's more about being truthful to what you are and also what you got from your family." But, of course, the ever-mercurial De Bayser does not follow in anyone's footsteps. "I like to play with heritage," he says, explaining how his game

of interiors can be played on material choices, by referencing the elegant soft yellow limestone cornices and architrave in a pair of sheep sculptures by François-Xavier Lalanne, for example. Elsewhere, the typically 19th-century ironwork and leaded rooftops visible outside are matched and contrasted inside. "I like the combination of totally new and fresh alongside old features and materials," he explains, gesturing toward a chunky, contemporary table he acquired from young French furniture designer Francesco Balzano: "You have to create tension."

With the trappings of a Parisian life all around, it is easy to overlook the fact that De Bayser currently spends the majority of his time in Berlin. This dual urban existence is another of the many paradoxes that he makes his own. Does the choice of a scaled-up, larger Parisian abode hint at homesickness—a desire to resettle on his home turf? "When I live 100 percent here, I get a little bit sick of Paris," he says. The past seven years have allowed De Bayser to regain a fondness, however. "I've started to like Paris more and more—almost as a tourist would." Not to say that he is tired of Berlin just yet: "Paris means all the tradition and culture, and Berlin means being more adventurous, a bit more experimental, daring even."

When creating beautiful homes in either the French or German capital, De Bayser's domestic endeavors seem removed from his professional life. The feeling that he has curated a sanctuary for himself using his personal taste pervades the apartment on rue de Monceau. "My day job is most definitely still The Corner Berlin, and it's a very big day job," he concedes. "Every day, you receive beautiful new collections and merchandise that you must show off and celebrate. It has to be crated, yes, but it's not a museum… I have to sell them."

Here, in the calm environment of a carefully crafted private space, perhaps the most obvious of the many contrasts of this entrepreneurial retailer-cum-furniture collector is clear. "The business side of my life is go-go-go," he says, gesticulating. "You receive things, you sell things, and so on." But, at home, as he reclines back on his Pierre Jeanneret couch, the therapeutic value of his passion for collecting—and keeping—interiors is self-evident. Perhaps, concludes De Bayser, work and home don't have to be countries apart: "I suppose it's all about proportions for me. It either fits or it doesn't fit."

A mirrored coffee table by Ron Arad is surrounded by pieces from Pierre Jeanneret, Jean Prouvé, Serge Mouille and Mathieu Matégot.

"*I've started to like Paris more and more—almost as a tourist would.*"

De Bayser's previous home in Paris (pictured throughout) comprised 650 square feet and also overlooked Parc Monceau in the 8th Arrondissement.

RED

Red hair, don't care: Celebrating the beauty of the ginger gene.

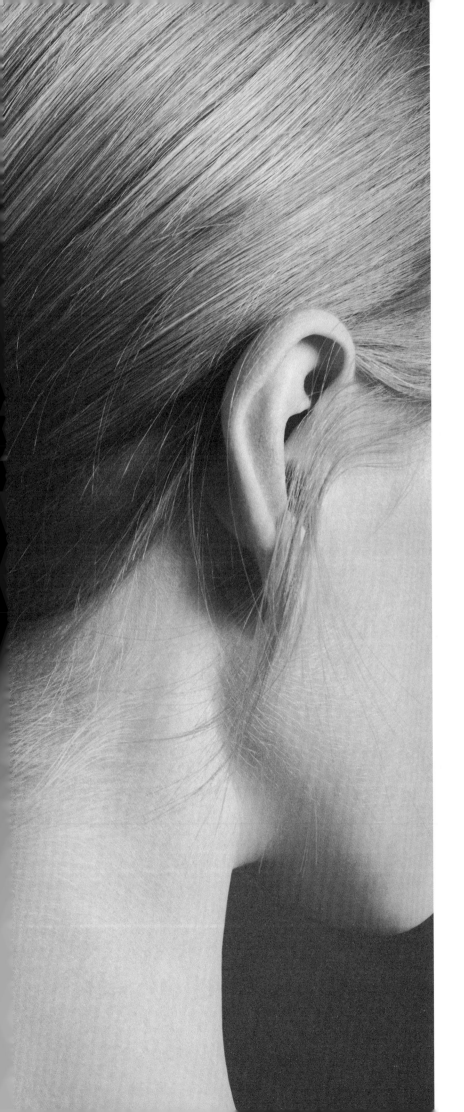

HEADS

Photography by Hasse Nielsen & Styling by Barbara Gullstein

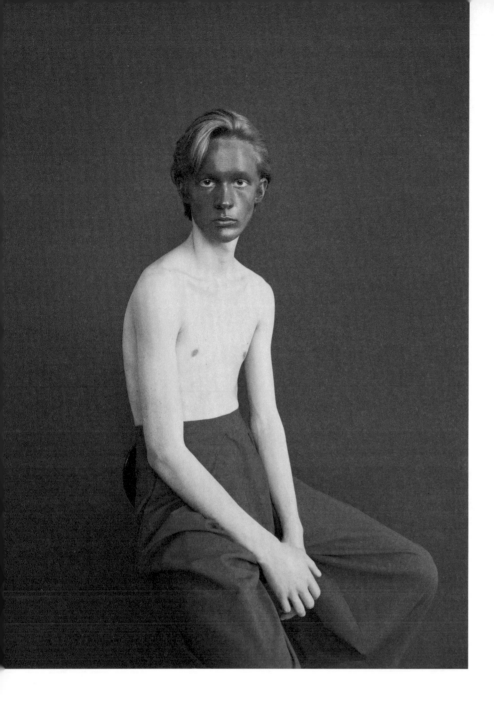

Above: Leo wears trousers by & Other Stories. Right: Ina and Lulu wear dresses by Anne Sofie Madsen.

Hair: Line Bille, Makeup: Ignacio Alonso

Previous: Lulu wears stylist's own vintage shirt. Left: She wears eye shadow from MAC Cosmetics.

Left: Lulu wears a coat by Rodebjer, sweatshirt by Acne Studios and boots by & Other Stories. Below: She wears stockings by Wolford.

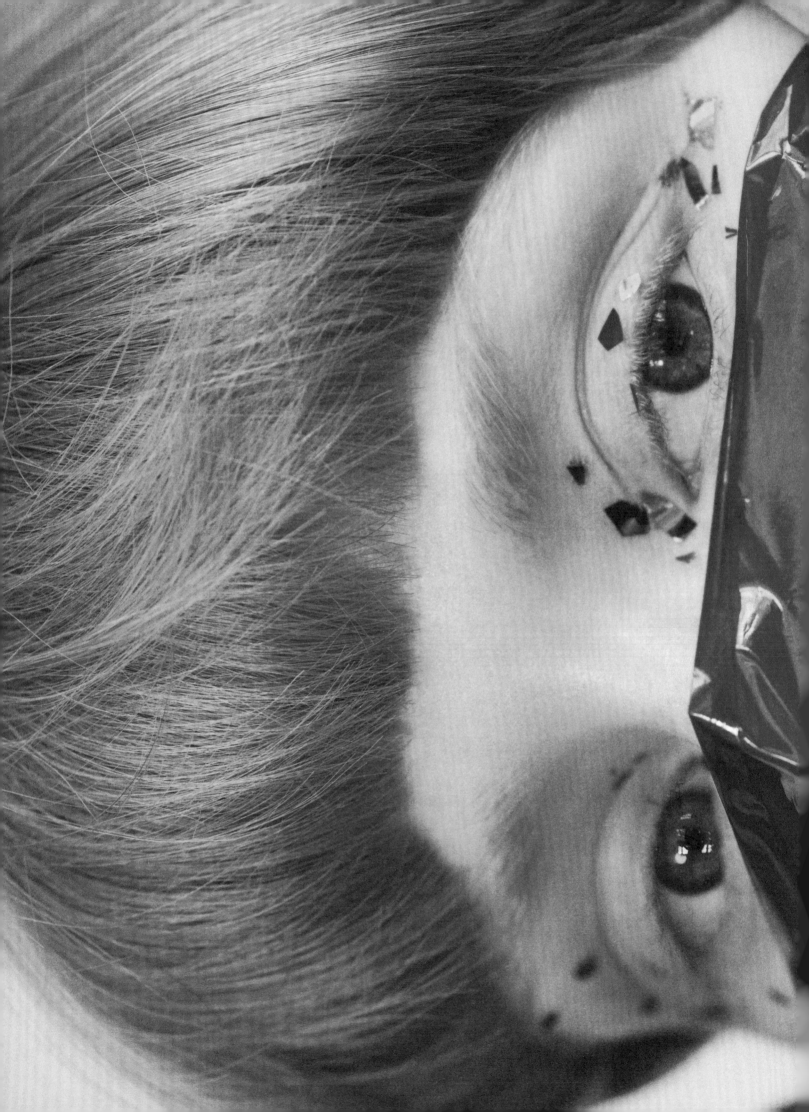

Right: Leo wears a suit by Mark Tan.

Going Solo:

In Defense of Loneliness

If the heart is a lonely hunter, as *Carson McCullers* wrote, what does it want? Certainly, one can be as lonely in a relationship as when single, as lonely at a party as when home on the couch. At a time in which social apps used to avoid loneliness often seem to only exploit and compound it, *Harriet Fitch Little* shines a light on one of life's most concealed emotions and examines how, by identifying loneliness as an inescapable hallmark of human experience, it might just be harnessed for good.

Living is hugely lonely. We are born alone and we will die alone, and the gap between us and those around us is insurmountable—however hard we try to bridge it with love and proximity.

This may seem a crushingly bleak statement with which to begin a conversation about loneliness. Please, don't abandon hope or interest. Because if understood correctly, this idea can be tremendously liberating: Rather than approaching loneliness as something that is either absent or present, we can approach it as a taxonomy of types. There are multiple ways to be lonely, and while some are deadly, others are empowering. As the poet Carl Sandburg once put it, when expounding nostalgically on the greatness of Shakespeare and Leonardo da Vinci, "They had loneliness and knew what to do with it."

There is a dearth of research on loneliness. This may be because it falls between two fields of inquiry; it isn't classified as a mental illness, so doctors overlook it, and it is by its very nature too antisocial to interest social scientists. Or maybe it's just too vilified an emotion for us to want to discuss: As *Generation X* author Douglas Coupland once wryly observed, "Forget sex or politics or religion, loneliness is the subject that clears out a room."

Those who have studied loneliness—the American social neuroscientist John Cacioppo is foremost among them—tend to understand it in blunt evolutionary terms. Cacioppo's influential thesis, set out in his book *Loneliness: Human Nature and the Need for Social Connection*, sees loneliness as a biological mechanism—a warning system that motivates us to repair deficient social relationships.

"The pain of loneliness is the response mechanism set up by our bodies telling us that we need that physical and emotional connection," says Dr. Kellie Payne, researcher for the UK-based charity Campaign to End Loneliness. Echoing Cacioppo's argument, Payne explains that our basic impulse as a species is to make sure we stick together to increase our likelihood of survival. The gut-churning horror of loneliness is a pain response set up to tell us when we're doing something damaging, similar to putting our hand on a hot stove and knowing we need to immediately pull it back.

The Campaign to End Loneliness is focused on mitigating the effects of loneliness in old age, when a confluence of factors—retirement, bereavement, lack of access to transportation and social activities—makes isolation a serious health risk. Payne reels off the negative consequences of loneliness that researchers have observed: People who identify as lonely are 50 percent more likely to die early, making it a more fatal condition than obesity. This is partly the result of poor health behaviors associated with isolation. If we are alone we have no one to eat well with, and no one to impress with our well-exercised body. More strikingly, research has shown that loneliness itself does physical damage. "What happens to your body when you're lonely is it goes into a state where you're more stressed. Your body releases stress hormones, and your sleep won't be as restorative," Payne says. A 2006 study from Northwestern University found that older adults who describe themselves as lonely wake with a pronounced jolt of cortisol—a hormone also associated with negative effects including depression and obesity. "It's a fight or flight thing. Your body finds comfort in having connections, and when you're isolated you're constantly on guard."

Payne draws a distinction between loneliness and solitude: Solitude is merely the objective state of being alone, whereas loneliness arises "when the connections that you want and the connections that you have are not the same." Understanding the pain that loneliness can cause doesn't mean dismissing solitude. Sara Maitland, feminist novelist and author of nonfiction titles including *A Book of Silence* and *How to Be Alone*, lives by herself in a cottage she built in the Scottish wilderness. Maitland explains that even though many people claim to draw a distinction between loneliness and solitude, the reality is that they often blur the two. In doing so, they attribute negative consequences to spending time alone when there might be none.

Maitland, who started living alone after a difficult divorce, lists the benefits she has reaped from solitude: "I am financially better off, I haven't lost any friendships, I'm happier than I've been in my life and I'm writing better and more originally."

She believes firmly that we are bred to think we need more connections than we really do. "Enormous efforts go into training little children to be sociable. It doesn't come naturally to them—'Don't bite,' 'Share your toys'—and they're not being simultaneously trained for solitude. I've never heard anyone say, 'Why don't you go to your room and stay there for a bit as a reward.'"

The solitude that Maitland advocates is of an exceptionally sociable stripe: She returned from a work trip in England the previous day; she spent the hour before our conversation on the phone with her daughter discussing her grandchild; she has a dog; she has neighbors who regularly check in on her; she is in constant contact with other happy loners because she helps organize retreats for them. In other words, her positive experience of solitude isn't the result of having no connections. To the contrary, it's the product of having a rich network of relationships while also having time alone to work on creative projects. It's reminiscent of Henry Thoreau, America's most celebrated naturalist, who famously lived alone in a woodland cabin by Walden Pond in Massachusetts... except that he would go to his mother to get his laundry done and frequently eat, drink and generally make merry in the nearby town.

Women have been historically denied the luxury of solitude because of the responsibilities of family; this is the argument that Virginia Woolf puts so eloquently in the seminal 1929 feminist text *A Room of One's Own*. Maitland is happy to agree: "There is a certain amount of social capital that you can bring into being alone that improves the experience for you." The story might end here. For all their points of contention, the bottom line in both Maitland and Payne's worldviews is that while solitude has the potential to be positive, loneliness categorically doesn't.

But it is hard not to wonder. Anyone who has taken up writing love poetry after a heartbreak, or started a diary following some significant upheaval, will have experienced firsthand the link between creative thoughts and lonely moments.

This is the territory that British author Olivia Laing explores, cautiously, in *The Lonely City: Adventures in the Art of Being Alone*. She tows the line on not romanticizing loneliness, writing with unvarnished honesty about the months she spent living alone in New York, eating cereal standing up and watching her hair fall out in clumps following a bad breakup in a city far from home. She was approaching her mid-30s, she recalls, and describes it bluntly as an age when loneliness "carries with it a persistent whiff of strangeness, deviance and failure."

And yet she is convinced that an emotion that so many people experience so strongly must merit a more serious treatment than we generally afford it. "Loneliness is by no means a wholly worthless experience," she insists. And it's hardly deviant. So universal is loneliness that to experience it is to be human, says Laing.

Along with personal reflections, Laing's book also delves into the relationship between loneliness and the creation of art.

One of the artists Laing considers at length is Henry Darger. Perhaps the most famous and enigmatic self-taught artist in the world, Darger lived a life of fairly unremitting isolation. He was institutionalized as a child, and spent his adult life working as a hospital porter in Chicago. In all that time, only one close friend passed through his life. Working in near-total isolation, he created an epic artistic oeuvre: a fantasy manuscript that ran to 15,145 typed pages, and almost 300 watercolor and collage illustrations that depicted strange scenes from the make-believe world of The Vivian Girls—sexually ambiguous children who were often pictured fighting men on horseback.

In the absence of human companionship, Darger plowed his emotions into creating an entire universe populated by a rich cast of friends and foes. But Laing pushes the argument further. She thinks that Darger used his art to address traumas in his life that would normally be unburdened on family and friends. His childhood was one of abuse and abandonment, and Laing thinks it is no coincidence that the recurrent theme in his work was violent wars being fought by children. "He dedicated his life to making images in which the forces of good and evil could be brought together in a single frame," she writes.

What Laing is hinting at is that loneliness can be a creative force in that it compels us to find, through art, the things we would otherwise seek out in people. Prison literature is a rich illustration of this idea—a large number of

"Enormous efforts go into training little children to be sociable... They're not being simultaneously trained for solitude. I've never heard anyone say, 'Why don't you go to your room and stay there for a bit as a reward.'"

canonical works have been written by authors behind bars. There are many reasons for this: Maitland would probably suggest it is simply a question of having time to think undisturbed; historians would add that famous books are often written by people with ideas that shocked at the time of writing, making a spell behind bars far more likely. I think we might add to this list the fact that loneliness breeds in us a desperate desire to substitute for the connections whose absence we feel most strongly. It is not a coincidence that Cervantes conceived of *Don Quixote*—a comic masterpiece about a knight roaming freely throughout Spain—while confined to a cell. Or that the notorious Marquis de Sade wrote *Justine*, his salacious tale of lust, while imprisoned with no access to women. Lonely people want to find substitutes for human company; this is a creative project that is missing in Maitland's understanding of happy solitude.

Laing is a politically astute writer. She explains that conversations about loneliness are often conversations about overlapping forms of marginalization and social exclusion. Writing about David Wojnarowicz, the American painter and photographer who was most active in New York in the 1980s, she discusses loneliness in the context of stigma. Wojnarowicz was gay and HIV positive, and these two things meant that he experienced adulthood as a series of aggressions and rejections. Cut off from conventional channels of communication, he turned to art: "[His] life was spent trying to escape solitary confinement of one kind or another, to figure a way out of the prison of the self," writes Laing. She goes on to place other seemingly very different artists at vari-

ous points on her map of loneliness, from Edward Hopper to Andy Warhol.

When we talk, she clarifies her overarching argument. "I don't want to romanticize it, but at the same time with the artists I'm looking at there's a strong sense that not being able to find a common language gave them a way to turn [communication] into a making of object or images."

Where does this leave us? Certainly not rushing to the hills. There is nothing in Laing's work that suggests a life of isolation is to be wished for. In fact, *The Lonely City* leaves a reader with a crystal-clear sense of why the figure of the self-consciously angsty art school student is so often a comical one: The creativity of loneliness can't come from enforced isolation, because lonely people want more desperately than anything to connect. It's an emotion of yearning that can't be counterfeited.

What is important to remember is that loneliness lives in everyone. Julia Bainbridge, who hosts *The Lonely Hour* podcast, tells me that there has been something "hugely comforting" in the more open conversations about loneliness that have been happening recently. From her home in Atlanta, she interviews writers, celebrities and family members about their experiences of angst and isolation. "A lot of people presume it's the episode where I interview my mother about alcoholism that meant the most to me, but actually it's the interviews with people who are further away who I didn't necessarily realize in advance were lonely," she says. For Bainbridge and her growing tribe of listeners, it is enough to know that other people are also very lonely for it to morph from a shameful

embarrassment to a potentially potent force. As she now happily admits: "I've done all my best work when I've been single and alone."

Both Laing and Bainbridge think that our normal reaction is to recoil from loneliness. We withdraw from those we sense it in, almost as if we might catch it, and when we identify it in ourselves we often work desperately to mask it—with bad relationships, nights out with people who aren't really friends, or even just the hum of voices from the TV.

But rather than rushing to paper over the cracks, Laing in particular believes it wiser that we learn to lean in slightly—to sit comfortably for a moment with our loneliness and that of others. In particular, she thinks we would benefit from spending time in the company of the artists, writers and deep thinkers who have made some headway in reaching out in the darkness, who have tried to stretch themselves across the divide that separates any one person from every other. What the evolutionary psychologists seem to forget in their haste to rationalize every ounce of our behavior is that so much of what is good and interesting about being human comes from our flair for creative problem-solving: If loneliness is a problem, the artistic solutions we have hit upon to help lessen it are surely worth exploring.

Laing thinks she's found a good accommodation: "It's not like the feeling of loneliness ended when I finished the book," she tells me. "But I'd sort of cracked it open in a way, and found things that were beautiful, meaningful and intellectually exciting inside." If loneliness is a populated city, it's about time we got to know our neighbors.

MICHAELA

AELA

The young ballerina dancing all over the stereotypes of a pressure-intense career.

Words by Djassi DaCosta Johnson & Photography by Ruby Woodhouse

"I want people to see the grit and the blood and everything I've really gone through."

Styling: Jordy Huinder, Hair & Makeup: Mascha Meyer

In 2014, Michaela wrote a memoir with the help of her mother. Titled *Taking Flight*, the book allowed her to narrate her childhood experiences.

A s an orphan growing up during Sierra Leone's brutal civil war, Michaela DePrince found a magazine blowing in the wind. On its cover was a ballerina and a new inspiration. Now, at the age of 22, Michaela is immersed in the world of ballet. She has also danced with Beyoncé, written a book, and is currently working on a movie based on her life. But hers is not a fairy tale. It is a story of resilience in the face of racism, diligence in honing raw talent and self-care in a world fixated on stereotypes.

Touring the world with the Dutch National Ballet, Michaela is living any ballet dancer's dream. But she is the only female dancer of color in the internationally renowned company and the first soloist of African descent. The world was introduced to Michaela in 2011 when she was one of six young dancers featured in the ballet documentary *First Position*. She was seen overcoming injury to perform spectacularly and win a scholarship to the American Ballet Theatre's Jacqueline Kennedy Onassis School of Ballet. Since then, she has performed with Lucent Dance Theater in the Netherlands, was the youngest member of the Dance Theatre of Harlem, performed with South African Ballet Theatre, and, in 2014 returned to the Netherlands to join the junior division of the Dutch National Ballet in Amsterdam. She was promoted to soloist in 2016.

Apart from her spectacular talent and rise to fame as a ballet superstar, Michaela has a harrowing story to tell of her early years. In 2014, she published a book, *Taking Flight*, soon to be adapted into a film, about her life in civil war-torn Sierra Leone before she was adopted into an American family at the age of five. Rebels are said to have killed her father, and shortly thereafter her mother died of fever and starvation. Michaela ended up in an orphanage. She was taunted and abused because she has vitiligo, a skin condition marked by white patches, which was considered a "curse of the devil." One of the more astonishing things about her journey is how much prejudice and racism she has had to endure in the culture of the ballet world. Her story is a reminder of the pure, unbridled passion and resilience it takes to be a professional dancer, and how many dancers, regardless of color, class or opportunity, are successful because of their unwavering dedication to the stage.

Now that you are a seasoned professional at the age of 22, what do you think is the biggest difference between being a student of ballet, and a professional ballet dancer working in a company? I realized when I got into the Dutch National Ballet that it's not all about having high legs, being the skinniest, doing big jumps or being able to do a million turns—it's about how you affect people when you dance. You can watch someone on stage and observe how the way they gesture moves you. That's the difference between being a student and being a professional; it's understanding how to refine things and think about details instead of just performing the movements.

How has growing up in America, and being subject to American racial and social structures, affected your drive as a dancer? It makes me so angry that we still have to talk about this. That it's still a fucking subject—pardon my French. I performed in London, and I'm just happy that they actually accepted me because I wore brown tights and it's been such a hassle to do that. I don't wear pink tights anymore. I will never, ever wear pink tights again. And I know people in the ballet world won't understand why I wear brown tights—that's fine—I don't really care if you don't choose to move forward but, come on... I've heard people say that it's "distracting" to see black dancers on stage. Well, if you had more then you wouldn't be so distracted.

But being in Europe has also given me the drive to talk about these things, because I thought it would be completely different here. People say that in Europe, people are more open-minded. I love my company, but it's only me. I'm the only black dancer. Except for Bruno Da Rocha Pereira, a dark-skinned Brazilian dancer. And then there's Precious Adams at the English National Ballet. Where are the others? It's really upsetting. Another thing that upsets me is that a lot of people don't hire more dark-skinned and black ballerinas in their company because they say, "Well, we already have a black or African-American girl." And that's fine, but why do you have only one? Get more. Get medium-, get darker-skinned. People are scared of change and being different, but I think it's beyond time to change things up.

Now that you've found a platform to share your story and inspire other young brown girls and boys who want to pursue ballet, or dance—or any of the fine arts for that matter—what do you see as your artistic trajectory? For me, it's about becoming the best artist I can possibly be. It's such a short career that I want to make sure that I grow and learn as much as I can in the time that I have.

Can we talk a little about overcoming injury and what you've learned in terms of self-care—mentally, physically, or even setting boundaries professionally? Setting boundaries is one of my biggest issues. Because again, I love to learn, but sometimes it can be too much on my body—I can only take so much "personal growth" at a time. I've been working on making more time to get to know myself. I've always taken care of other people, my friends and family. I never wanted to fully "know myself" because I wasn't sure I'd like what I would find, I guess. But I'm learning that I'm pretty okay. I'm not that bad!

What are some of your most unforgettable performances? When I performed in South Africa, I danced the role of Kitri in Don Quixote with Joburg Ballet. Before I went on, I relaxed by lying on the floor, kind of taking a little bit of a nap. It was my last show there, and I weirdly felt an almost out-of-body experience. And it was one of my best performances! I was relaxed; I was in the role; I wasn't putting pressure on myself. I got to enjoy every single moment and was just having so much fun on stage. It was as if I was Kitri.

How important are relationships and trust building? On and off the stage, what relationships have been most important in supporting your career? I've had some bad relationships and have been hurt a few times, so it's taken me a while to realize that I don't need a lot of friends, I just need good ones. I now have a really nice group of friends at the ballet, and we have a blast inside and outside the studio. We talk about what we want to do after dancing, about ballet, about politics and what's going on in the world, about what's meaningful for us right now.

"I've heard people say that it's 'distracting' to see black dancers on stage. Well, if you had more then you wouldn't be so distracted."

Michaela wears a leotard by Wolford, trousers by David Laport and shoes by COS.

Left: Michaela wears a turtleneck by Peet Dullaert, trousers by Wolford, earrings by Sophie Buhai and shoes by COS.
Below: She wears a dress by David Laport and shoes by COS.

What do you envision for the future of the classical ballet world, artistically and otherwise? I would love to really just see more diversity before I retire: different colors, different body types. It does seem to be happening, but slowly. One of my favorite sayings is, "Never be afraid to be a poppy in a sea of daffodils." So, let's have more poppies!

I'd love if you'd talk a little about your experience filming the Beyoncé video. How do you think your presence in a huge pop culture "statement video" can improve the visibility of classical ballet? Besides being an incredible experience, filming with Beyoncé gave me an opportunity to reach out to a younger crowd. Maybe they don't realize they can make it in the dance world, or maybe they don't know anything about ballet. The opportunity to portray ballet in a Beyoncé video was incredible.

What do you do outside of work and dance to recharge and refuel? Any hobbies or personal practices that you have developed? I'm blogging right now. Letting people know me in a different way. I recently announced on my blog that I have post-traumatic stress disorder [due to her experiences in Sierra Leone] because I've had friends in ballet—especially gay friends—who have also been affected by the way they were treated when they were younger. I wanted people to know that you have to talk to people when bad things happen in your life and just don't isolate yourself.

Is there something on the horizon that you're looking forward to? Yes! There are so many amazing things going on! There's a movie being created about my life, based on my book. We have an incredible director, and I'm involved with the script so that people get to know more of the "in-betweens." Because I know it can seem like a fairy tale, but I want people to see the grit and the blood and everything I've really gone through.

People often see dance—particularly ballet—as a short career. How long do you envision dancing and do you foresee a family and children in your future? I definitely want to have a family. I would like to have four kids, maybe adopt two. Maybe I'll dance until I'm 35 or 40—that's pushing it because I also want to do a lot of other things. I want to study human rights, to do something completely outside of the arts and just get to know myself better. I have much more to offer in this world. So, we'll see.

MORE MOVEMENT

by Djassi DaCosta Johnson

In 2015, Misty Copeland was named the first black principal female dancer at the American Ballet Theatre. This was a huge moment in ballet history. When George Balanchine came from Russia to form the School of American Ballet and later, the American Ballet Theatre in New York, his vision was for an integrated dance company. This vision was never realized. Arthur Mitchell was the first black dancer in the company in 1956 and others have been few and far between since then. Raven Wilkinson performed with the Ballet Russe in the 1950s (and was famously asked to use lighter makeup on her skin to "blend" and appear white). Other notable black ballerinas have been sprinkled across international stages over the years, including Janet Collins, Virginia Johnson, Aesha Ash and Lauren Anderson (a favorite idol of Michaela's). Michaela joins that list and a new era in classical ballet, in which darker-skinned dancers continue to blaze new trails and, finally, take center stage.

Archive:
Monir Shahroudy
Farmanfarmaian

In Tehran, *Monir Shahroudy Farmanfarmaian* reigns as the doyenne of contemporary Iranian art. Only at the age of 93, however, has her work found a permanent home: her own museum—the first in Iran dedicated to a solo female artist. She reflects on her life and career with *Charles Shafaieh.*

'I imagined myself standing inside a many-

Retirement has little attraction for Monir Shahroudy Farman-farmaian, the 93-year-old grande dame of Iranian contemporary art. At her Tehran studio, she leads a small team of men who help her to design and construct her mirror mosaic sculptures, many of which are now in the permanent collections of arts institutions worldwide, such as The Guggenheim in New York City and the Victoria and Albert Museum in London. She has a diverse oeuvre—drawing, textiles, jewelry, collages, memory boxes and even pieces done with the help of honeybees. But Farmanfarmaian is most lauded for her singular neotraditionalist innovations of a centuries-old Iranian artistic practice in which tiny pieces of glass, some colored by hand, are set together onto plaster in predetermined geometric patterns. The resulting works, from small mirror spheres (inspired by watching young children playing soccer) to large decagons and triangles, shimmer with dazzling surfaces, refracting the light and painting their surroundings with glittering, fragmentary reflections.

This effect evokes a foundational experience for Farmanfarmaian's art. "In the late 1950s, I went to Shiraz with Robert Morris and Marcia Hafif and took them to the Shah-e-Cheragh shrine," she writes from Tehran, recalling that transcendent event shared with her friends, two of America's preeminent minimalist artists. The Shia funerary shrine and mosque, whose name roughly translates to "King of Light," is renowned for its interior comprised of millions of small pieces of mirrored glass. As

she describes in her 2007 memoir, *A Mirror Garden*, co-written with Zara Houshmand, "the very space seemed on fire, the lamps blazing in hundreds of thousands of reflections. I imagined myself standing inside a many-faceted diamond and looking out at the sun…It was a universe unto itself, architecture transformed into performance, all movement and fluid light, all solids fractured and dissolved in brilliance, in space, in prayer. I was overwhelmed." At that point, she began contemplating bringing this experience, usually relegated to palaces and religious sites, to the homes of Iranians and others alike.

A decade later, a serendipitous encounter led to her first mirror-based pieces. In Tehran, her husband's friend was decorating his house with mirror work, and when she went to visit the construction site, she met Hajj Ostad Navid, a master artisan leading the project. Though Farmanfarmaian had to beg Hajj Ostad Navid to convince him that he should help a woman in her artistic endeavors, he eventually acquiesced. And they had a fruitful partnership that was instrumental in realizing the designs Farmanfarmaian had first conjured in dreams. This initial chauvinistic response has repeated itself throughout her career, but she does not dwell. She says, "the master I hired after coming back to Tehran in 2004 did not want to work with me either, but he got used to me. It has been difficult sometimes, to work with men who think that women are not very knowledgeable, but over time, they've understood that perhaps I do have some sense of art

and design." Farmanfarmaian's life has been punctuated by many other serendipitous encounters. Born in 1924 in Qazvin, she attended the University of Tehran's Fine Arts College but left quickly out of a desire for a different education. She was determined to go to Paris, inspired by a French professor who had shown works by Gauguin and others to her and her classmates. But in 1944, the Second World War made such travel impossible. So instead she took a circuitous three-month journey to America (with documentation stating she was a nurse) via India and Australia, facilitated by Donald Wilber, a scholar of Iranian history. She found out much later that Wilber was also a CIA operative who helped mount the 1953 Iranian coup d'état that reinstalled the Shah.

"I arrived in New York City in 1945 and stayed for over 12 years," she says. Studying first at Cornell University and later at the Parsons School of Design, Farmanfarmaian "met many American artists—Jackson Pollock, Mark Rothko, Willem de Kooning, Joan Mitchell, Frank Stella and Andy Warhol." A number of these connections occurred at the Eighth Street Club and the Cedar Tavern in Greenwich Village, notable artistic haunts. Art critics often insist on finding continuity between Farmanfarmaian's work and these abstract expressionists and pop artists, but she withholds comment on their possible aesthetic ties. "I did not consider myself an artist back then. The connections I made were on a personal level rather than an artistic one."

Previous spread: Monir at home in Tehran in 1975. Right: The artist and her relief work in the 1970s.

faceted diamond and looking out at the sun.'

A notable exception was Milton Avery, a successor to Matisse and friend of Rothko's and other abstract expressionists. As with so many of Farmanfarmaian's friendships, an element of luck was crucial to their meeting, though her warm and playful personality—on full display in Bahman Kiarostami's recent documentary *Monir*—no doubt helped. "Milton was one of my neighbors in Woodstock, where I would rent a cottage every summer while living in New York," she recalls. "He would walk over to my home and make drawings. He was very good and taught me to make monotypes. When I returned to Iran, my first exhibition in 1958 was of monotype flowers based on the technique I learned from him." That same year, those pieces would win a gold medal at the Venice Biennale.

"I'm a visual person," she says. "I always look for things to marvel at, be they found in nature or in art." After Farmanfarmaian returned to Iran in 1956 following her second marriage, it was her encounters traveling across the country that molded her principal aesthetics. In part, these excursions related to her job for the Point Four program, a Marshall Plan initiative that entailed positioning traditional Iranian crafts for foreign markets. "In the 1970s," she says, "I took many trips to the countryside and bought Qajar coffeehouse paintings, stained glass windows, Safavid doors, hand-carved Turkoman jewelry and other folk art from houses scheduled for destruction—in order to preserve this heritage." Her exhaustive collection was seized during the revolution, however, along with her contemporary art. She had gifts from Alexander Calder and others, including a Warhol "Marilyn Monroe" that still has her address on its back and was recently sold at Sotheby's.

While Farmanfarmaian rarely elaborates on her own work, she explains its basic foundations. "I start with the point, which opens up to the circle," she says. "From there, you can divide the circle into three points to a triangle, four points to a square, five to a pentagon, and all the way up to 12-sided forms." An underlying structure to much of her work is her system of infinite possibility, of shapes divided into an endless series of other shapes, which draws upon the complex cosmology of the Sufi tradition in Islam. Farmanfarmaian is less driven by philosophical theories than many of her peers, including other geometry-minded artists like Piet Mondrian. "My work explores the relation between arcane symbols and geometrical shapes. For example, the triangle represents human consciousness, the square the four directions, and 12 is the zodiac—the 12 stars in the universe."

While Josef Albers loved squares, Farmanfarmaian focuses on the hexagon. She has previously explained that the shape has "many meanings. Its six sides can be representative of the directions: forward, backward, right, left, up, and down; as well as the six virtues: generosity, self-discipline, patience, determination, insight and compassion." Ubiquitous in Persian art and architecture, from mosques to carpets, hexagons also attract Farmanfarmaian for their ease of divisibility and the gapless bonds they form with each other.

Drawing has always been a central part of Farmanfarmaian's work, though for decades her drawings were ignored as secondary to her mirror work. In fact, in 1953 she drew the original Persian violet that was used as the symbol of Bonwit Teller, the celebrated New York department store. She was paid all of $150 for it by an agent who didn't disclose his client's name. Interestingly, she was actually working for Bonwit Teller at the time as a layout designer (and had befriended a co-worker, Andy Warhol). Now to Farmanfarmaian's delight, her works on paper receive attention not as mere preparatory sketches or idle doodles but as an independent body of work. Featuring just colored felt-tip markers or a Chinese brush, they take on a freer form.

"It's been difficult sometimes, to work with men who think that women aren't very knowledgeable."

Above: Monir working in her Tehran studio on a sculpture that she later titled *Heptagon Star* in 1975.

The Monir Museum opened in
December 2017 in Tehran, at the city's
Negarestan Garden. It displays 51 of
Farmanfarmaian's works.

"My flower drawings, in particular, are much less premeditated," she says. "The lines are almost calligraphic, and I let them flow unselfconsciously, often unbroken from start to finish."

Other geometric drawings, related in form to her mirror work, are more regimented but exude a sense of freedom and sprightliness impossible in her sculptures. Though flat, these abstract works' coloration and often sheer profusion of lines and shapes create the illusion of three dimensions.

Drawing was a medium in which Farmanfarmaian could work without assistants while exiled in New York City following the revolution. This was also the period when she created her *Heartaches* memory box series, filled with family photographs and other personal ephemera, following the death of her husband in 1991.

Though she spent decades abroad, by choice and not, exile does not define her work. It is Iranian in the sense that Farmanfarmaian has preserved some classical artistic traditions, but this is not her primary concentration. Similarly—with the exception of *Lightning for Neda* (2009), a gargantuan six-panel mirror mosaic that memorializes Neda Agha-Soltan who was killed during the 2009 election protests in Iran—Farmanfarmaian's work is not an overt commentary on the current regime. Rather, all who confront her mirrors are abstracted, made diffuse, unrecognizable and, in a way, equal. The spectator becomes subsumed within, consumed by, and multiplied, inside and outside the piece as each mosaic endlessly metamorphoses with the changing light. In this reflected and reflective space, there are neither veils nor nudity, and no elements of power or authority, religious or otherwise. In their constant fluidity, the mirror works reside solely in the present. The reflective glass fragments fracture and explode the viewer in mystifying, unpredictable, and thus challenging ways. As the late Iranian filmmaker and photographer Abbas Kiarostami commented, "We have become indifferent to introspection and thoughts about the world around us. Standing before Monir's mirrors, unable to see our own image, we are forced to take an inner journey."

Farmanfarmaian still feels the compulsion to create. She often repeats that she remains "on a constant quest for the new." Now, after enduring the relocation or destruction of many of her monumental works, she has received an honor at home that supersedes those from galleries and museums elsewhere. In December 2017, she presided over the opening of a museum in Tehran dedicated to her work. With more than 50 pieces from her private collection, the Monir Museum, housed in a 19th-century palace, is a landmark event, both for Farmanfarmaian and Iranian political and cultural history. As she points out, with quiet pride and likely a small hidden smile, "It is the first museum in the country dedicated to a woman artist."

Mirrorwork and reverse glass painting is the hallmark of Monir's practice. The three works pictured (left to right: *Nonagon, Triangle, Pentagon*) were created in 2013, when the artist was in her late 80s.

Foe

& Dear

113 — 176

Paris

MÉTRO

Insouciance. Candor. Youth. The enduring appeal of Nouvelle Vague.

BOULOT

Photography by Annie Lai & Styling by Kingsley Tao

DISCO

Previous spread: Elliot wears a jacket, shirt and trousers by Margaret Howell, vest by Xander Zhou and shoes by John Lobb. Above and right:
He wears a shirt by Margaret Howell, coat by Xander Zhou, trousers by Band of Outsiders and shoes by John Lobb.

Above: Elliot wears a coat by Mackintosh, shirt by Margaret Howell, trousers by Zander Zhou and shoes by John Lobb.
Kat wears a coat and shoes by A.F. Vandevorst and a dress by Bora Aksu.

Right: Kat wears a blouse, skirt and shoes by Rejina Pyo.

Left and below: Kat wears a dress by Loewe and earrings by Dinny Hall. Elliot wears a shirt and trousers by Xander Zhou, a belt by Gucci and shoes by John Lobb.

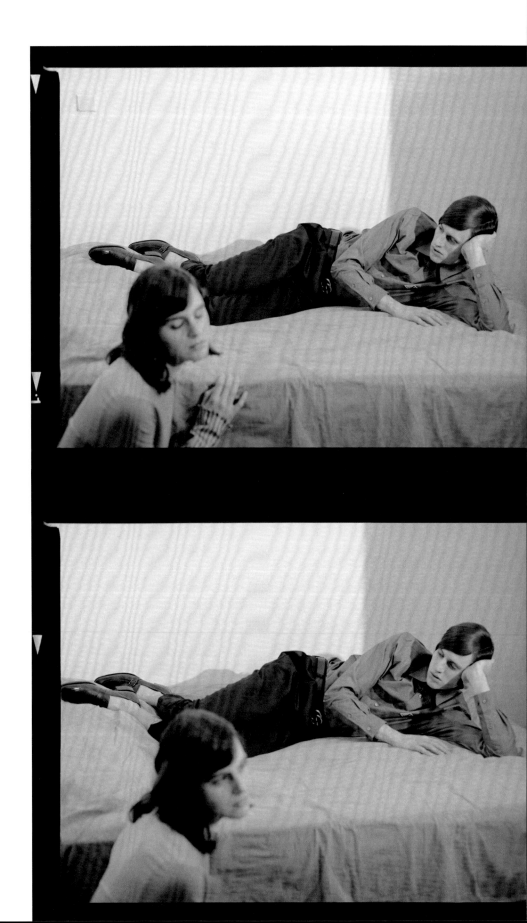

Above: Kat wears a top by Rejina Pyo and skirt by Toga Archives. Elliot wears a shirt by Loewe. Right: He wears a shirt by Xander Zhou.

Hair & Makeup: Jonathan Sanchez, Makeup: Khela

Left: Elliot wears a coat by Mackintosh, a shirt by Margaret Howell and trousers by Xander Zhou. Kat wears a jacket
and shoes by A.F. Vandevorst, a dress by Bora Aksu and a necklace by Cornelia Webb.

Photography by *Kira Bunse & Osma Harvilahti*

P A R
U N
G U I

Words by *Haydée Touitou & Pip Usher*

I S :

D E .

From a feng shui swimming pool and cramped bookshop to a ceramist's studio and modernist's dream apartment, we explore the hidden gems of Paris.

Pierre Touitou

Pierre Touitou, the 24-year-old chef behind charming Parisian bistro Vivant, is just the type of floppy-haired man-about-town that you might hope would show you his city.

"The weekend is about love, rest and parties... and you never know what will be the priority," he says, without clarifying further. After closing up at his lively 25-seat restaurant, where he can be found conjuring up simple plates of Sardinian pasta behind the bar's marble counter, Pierre heads a few doors down to Hôtel Bourbon, a club that prides itself on being the stomping ground of the city's bright young things. The following day, lunch at seafood restaurant Clamato dusts away cocktail-induced cobwebs, after which Pierre heads to Champ Libre, his favorite flower shop, to prepare for the week ahead. "I spend a couple of hours rearranging the flower setup at Vivant while listening to some loud music," he says. Pierre enjoys going out to restaurants as much as he enjoys manning his own. Childhood haunt Marché Raspail, an organic Sunday market which boasts stalls of gleaming produce, is a nostalgic spot to check out what's in season. From there, he recommends a short wander over to narrow sushi bar Tsukizi, also in the 6th Arrondissement and a favorite with Pierre due to its "perfectly executed" fish. When night falls, conclude your gastronomic tour at Capitaine, a new restaurant from Pierre's former colleague, chef Baptiste Day.

Should you fail to secure a table? There's only one thing to do: Make like a Parisian and curse with passion. "The best advice I can give to someone who's visiting Paris for the first time is to say PUTAIN! all day long, to anyone," says Pierre, a "strong believer" that France's most prolifically used swear word captures the capital's spirit in two clipped syllables. "That word inspires me in the best and the worst of ways."

Words by Haydée Touitou

Words by Pip Usher

Visiting Michael Fink is like visiting a curmudgeonly uncle with a hoarding disorder; you can barely see his diminutive figure behind the endless piles of books and magazines, and any question you ask is met by a great heaving sigh. At Comptoir de l'Image, Fink's tiny shop focusing on photo books and collectible magazines, truculence is armor and bibliomania a talent. He has been running the business since 1993, and deeply loves every one of the two thousand editions that the shop has to offer. A quick glance at a stack of back issues of *Vogue Paris*, for example, and Fink could tell you which guest editors he does or doesn't have in stock: "I don't have Polanski anymore, but you might find the Orson Welles one at the bottom of the pile." Located at 44 Rue de Sévigné, in the heart of the historic Marais district, Comptoir de l'Image is a perfect pit stop between Musée Carnavalet and Galerie Perrotin, or between Musée Picasso and Maison Européenne de la Photographie.

Comptoir de l'Image

Marie-France Cohen

"I was out on Sunday and there was a family that was so stylish: a little girl with the most adorable coat, a woman who was wearing a men's black coat and her husband, who had long hair," says Marie-France Cohen. "I don't know who they were, but they were terribly inspiring."

So begins a glimpse into a Paris filled with easy elegance and beauty on every boulevard. Born in Aix-en-Provence to an aristocratic family, Marie-France is an unabashed aesthete who has built an empire on her appreciation for such detail. After she and her late husband launched beloved children's label Bonpoint in 1975, the pair became leading figures in Paris' elite fashion and design circles. Their status was cemented when they went on to establish concept store Merci in the fashionable Marais district in 2009.

With such sensibilities, it's no surprise to learn that Marie-France is a discerning shopper. Dries Van Noten is a favorite, whereas Céline is enjoyed in moderation ("some nice stuff, but they're just dreadfully expensive"). Historic department store Le Bon Marché is another frequent destination, allowing Marie-France to stay informed about what's en vogue. But despite her interest in new brands, her own wardrobe favors simplicity, quality materials and flattering cuts.

"If you only look good in certain shapes and proportions, then you allow yourself to go out of fashion," she says.

This exacting eye extends to another Parisian obsession: food. Marie-France loves her son's Italian restaurant, Pizza Chic, a Saint-Germain-des-Prés eatery which serves pizzas "made with the best mozzarella and olive oil" to the neighborhood's well-heeled clientele. Other favorites include Blueberry, an upmarket Japanese restaurant known for its creative sushi. "The décor is very nice," she declares. "I'll always tell you about décor. I can hardly have a good time if the décor is not nice." Widowed shortly after Merci's

inception, Marie-France eventually bid adieu to the emporium in favor of a much smaller boutique. Disheartened by the empty commercialism of big brands—"No beauty, no meaning, nothing"— she decided to create a graceful space stocked with homeware items of enduring appeal. After settling on a tiny 19th-century bistro, she filled it with ceramics, velvet cushions and other soft furnishings. The boutique's anti-trend, pro-beauty ethos is firmly emphasized in its name, Démodé, which translates to "out of fashion."

Despite decades in Paris, Marie-France still speaks with wonder of its cobbled passages and grand architecture. The weekend

markets, packed with fresh produce and sensational food, always prove inspiring for her, as do the city's smaller art museums, which often fly under the radar of tourists and Parisians alike. "Don't rush where you've been told to go," she says, insisting that newcomers instead prioritize a good pair of walking shoes and a relaxed itinerary. "Let yourself discover. There are so many little streets, so many beautiful buildings."

In the City of Light, luminous beauty is everywhere. All one needs to do is pay attention. "French people always complain... But when you wake up in the morning and cross la Seine, it's hard to believe how beautiful it is."

Aquazena

Though it might be gray outside, it's perennially sunny in Aquazena. "It's the first feng shui swimming pool in France, perhaps even in the world," explains Simon Despouys, the director of the public swimming pool. Visitors may feel they have entered a parallel dimension when they arrive at the center in Issy-les-Moulineaux, just outside of Paris: There are almost no right angles in the entire building, and its concrete walls have been tinted a shade of blue reminiscent of the Caribbean Sea. Its architects, Selma and Salwa Mikou, made every effort to invite natural light into the building; rounded windows recessed into the walls and ceilings amplify the sun's rays, which splash across swimmers and overhanging palm trees. Absent is the suffocating smell of chlorine (the water is ozone-treated), making the swimming, cardio practice or sauna experience one of clarity and brightness. "We also have a hammam, two squash courts and a tank featuring fish exclusively from Lake Malawi," adds Despouys.

After Madoka Rindal had her first child, she would wander the hillsides of the Parc des Buttes-Chaumont in Paris' 19th Arrondissement trying to lull her son to sleep. The sprawling public park—home to an artificial lake, grotto and countless winding paths—became so intimately familiar to Madoka that even now, years later, it feels like home. Afterward, she would head to Le Marigny, a simple café facing the entrance of the park. It's the type of place, she says, where old people have their habits and will talk about the weather, or where locals gossip with the waiter. After ordering a croque madame campagne (a grilled ham and cheese sandwich adorned with an egg) and tea with milk, the ceramist would grab a window seat and sink gently into her surroundings.

"I try to be as invisible as I can," she says of her café habits. "I watch people passing by on the street outside and imagine their lives, I listen to people's conversations, and, at a certain point, I dream away into my thoughts… After time spent in a café, I will always feel peaceful and come out with ideas for making or doing things." Inspiration also comes from the corners of Paris that sit outside the city's most fashionable districts. Madoka's several years spent in Chateau Rouge, a neighborhood known locally as the African Quarter, are still vivid. "There are a lot of African groceries, hairdressers, street peddlers selling fruits you've never seen, steamed corn, grilled corn, perfume, huge Chanel logo patterned blankets, and lots of people walking in every direction," she says. Her own life at that time mirrored the potent energy of life on the streets outside: It was a "dense and intense" existence, punctuated by frequent parties and alcohol-fueled discussions that went late into the night. Although brief, those years left an enduring mark on her relationship with the city.

"Paris has forced me to ask myself what exactly my identity is," she says. "In this city, there are so many different influences and even more creative people. You really need to know who you are, otherwise you get lost in the stream and become a bad imitation of someone else."

Madoka Rindal

Florence Lopez

Words by Haydée Touitou

Florence Lopez lives in an apartment unlike any other. It is hers, but also, theoretically, yours, for most of the furniture and objects here are for sale. Lopez, an antiquarian, has been welcoming clients up four flights of stairs and into her apartment at Rue du Dragon in the 6th Arrondissement for over 25 years. What happens to the space once an item is sold? Lopez redesigns the interior biannually, or whenever a major piece is carted away. Today, the color scheme is dominated by shades of blue and green; a bed frame by George Nakashima abuts several Brazilian pieces from the 1950s, including a coffee table by Giuseppe Scapinelli. Indeed, the main wall is evocative of the designs of Roberto Burle Marx, a landscape architect whose work caught Lopez's eye during a recent trip to Brazil. The next redesign of the space will take place in 2018.

Words by Haydée Touitou

Musée Zadkine

In the heart of Montparnasse, down a narrow path that leads between two buildings, is Musée Zadkine—the home and atelier of the late Russian-born sculptor Ossip Zadkine. The artist lived and worked here between 1928 and 1967 with his wife, the Algerian-born painter Valentine Prax. Today, thanks to an endowment from Prax, the building is dedicated to Zadkine's sculptures and life story. He worked in wood, stone, concrete, plaster and bronze, and over 300 of his pieces are on display in the museum. The living quarters are also open to the public, lending the museum a sense of warmth and intimacy.

PAPER

Better known for printing silk scarves, Hermès also prints a playful magazine.

PLANES

Words by Pip Usher & Photography by Ruby Woodhouse

High fashion and lighthearted fun—c'est impossible, non? Not on the glossy pages of *Le Monde d'Hermès*, a biannual magazine published by the Parisian fashion house. Take the most recent cover, which gathers together a cacophony of objects—cloth-cutting scissors, silk scarves, a solitary bicycle wheel—on a dream catcher–like structure that hangs suspended.

This gentle sense of playfulness filters through the inner pages of the magazine too, from the fashion photography to the abrupt discovery, halfway through, that the page orientation flips upside down. With a current circulation of 600,000 copies per issue and translations into 13 languages, the magazine has become a collector's item. It offers another portal into Hermès' cultured sphere, a space in which readers can disappear into the wild landscapes and outlandish illustrations that crawl across the pages. "Since the beginning, the goal has always remained the same: to express the personality of Hermès without taking ourselves too seriously, with creativity, optimism, diversity, lightness and audacity," says Hermès' artistic director, Pierre-Alexis Dumas.

A descendant of founder Thierry Hermès, Pierre-Alexis has a fashion lineage as immaculate as the house's leather goods. He joined the family firm in 1995 and was named as artistic director two decades later. Though the brand is part of his DNA, he's loath to assume an air of entitlement. "Even if I am part of the family, I'm still learning about Hermès every day." He is quick to add that his heritage alone will not ensure the business's success. Each collection comes with a weighty responsibility: "You have to bring something new, as every earlier generation did so impressively and inspiringly."

By Pierre-Alexis' telling, the magazine was a childhood dream of his late father. Jean-Louis Dumas, a shrewd businessman who transformed the fashion house from a local treasure into a global powerhouse in the '80s, had always harbored visions of launching his own publication; *Le Monde d'Hermès*, Pierre-Alexis says, is the realization of that fantasy. "It is an opportunity to express what Hermès is with humor and originality."

Pierre-Alexis' most recent editor's letter continues to lay out this creative manifesto in no uncertain terms: "Accomplished. Assertive. Authentic. Beautiful. Bold. Carré," it declares, going on to list, in alphabetical order, an array of attributes that describe the fashion house and its singular approach to crafting objects (the theme of the issue). While the ensuing editorial stays loosely related to the brand, it roams from musings on the safety pin's iconic role in fashion to an interview with the Japanese founder of an avant-garde magazine dedicated to objects. Pierre-Alexis attributes a large part of *Le Monde d'Hermès*' success to this editorial eclecticism.

"Every season, *Le Monde d'Hermès* invites the reader to discover the house's new collection of objects," says Pierre-Alexis. But he insists that each issue of the magazine is conceived as a stand-alone editorial piece without dictates from marketing. Such autonomy allows the team to cherry-pick their contributors, some of whom are lesser-known names who offer an unexpected perspective.

"We like to encourage collaborations with new talents such as photographers, reporters and writers, rather than working with established contributors who are already well-known," he says. "For instance, for the cover of the 2012 issue (Volume II), where the inside story was dedicated to silk, we worked with the photographer Olivia Bee. At the time, she was only 18 years old and was spotted through her blog which featured romantic and poetic photos, intimate but universal, about her daily life with her friends in Portland, Oregon. For Hermès, she recreated her own world out of silk."

While Hermès has always signified status, the magazine celebrates its products in contexts that ditch ultra-luxury in favor of surprise. Silk scarves, artfully cut clothing and buttery-soft leather accessories are framed in unusual landscapes—like a recent photo shoot in Amsterdam's Rijksmuseum library. Hidden amidst dusty volumes and hung from maroon wrought-iron railings, Hermès' patterned silks and dainty pocketbooks match the grandeur of the surroundings, while adding a hint of humor. "We like to play with our objects," says Pierre-Alexis.

And, despite the lure of digitalization, he remains adamant that a print edition serves his clientele's desires better. "There is a special pleasure in touching the paper it is printed on," he says, his appreciation of tactility reflecting Hermès' history of handcrafting leather goods. "We hope that the readers will always take as much pleasure in reading it as we do in creating it."

"Le Monde d'Hermès is an opportunity to express what Hermès is with humor and originality."

Pierre-Alexis Dumas took over the editorial leadership of Hermès' biannual magazine from his father, whose vision was to approach fashion editorials with frankness and originality.

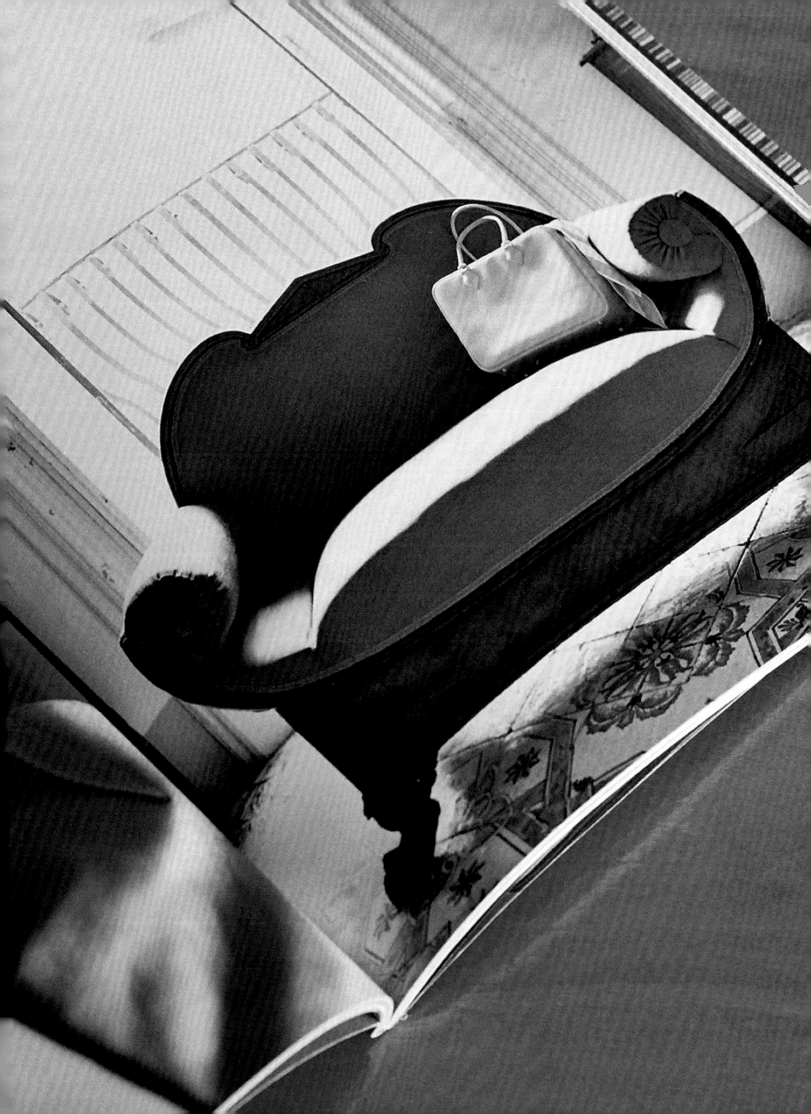

Words by *David Plaisant* & Photography by *Marsý Hild Þórsdóttir*

Day in The Life:
Ramdane Touhami

Once homeless on the streets of Paris, entrepreneur *Ramdane Touhami* now presides over some of the city's finest addresses with his beauty empire, Officine Universelle Buly.

The second outpost of Officine Universelle Buly is located in the Marais foundry where Auguste Rodin's *The Thinker* was cast.

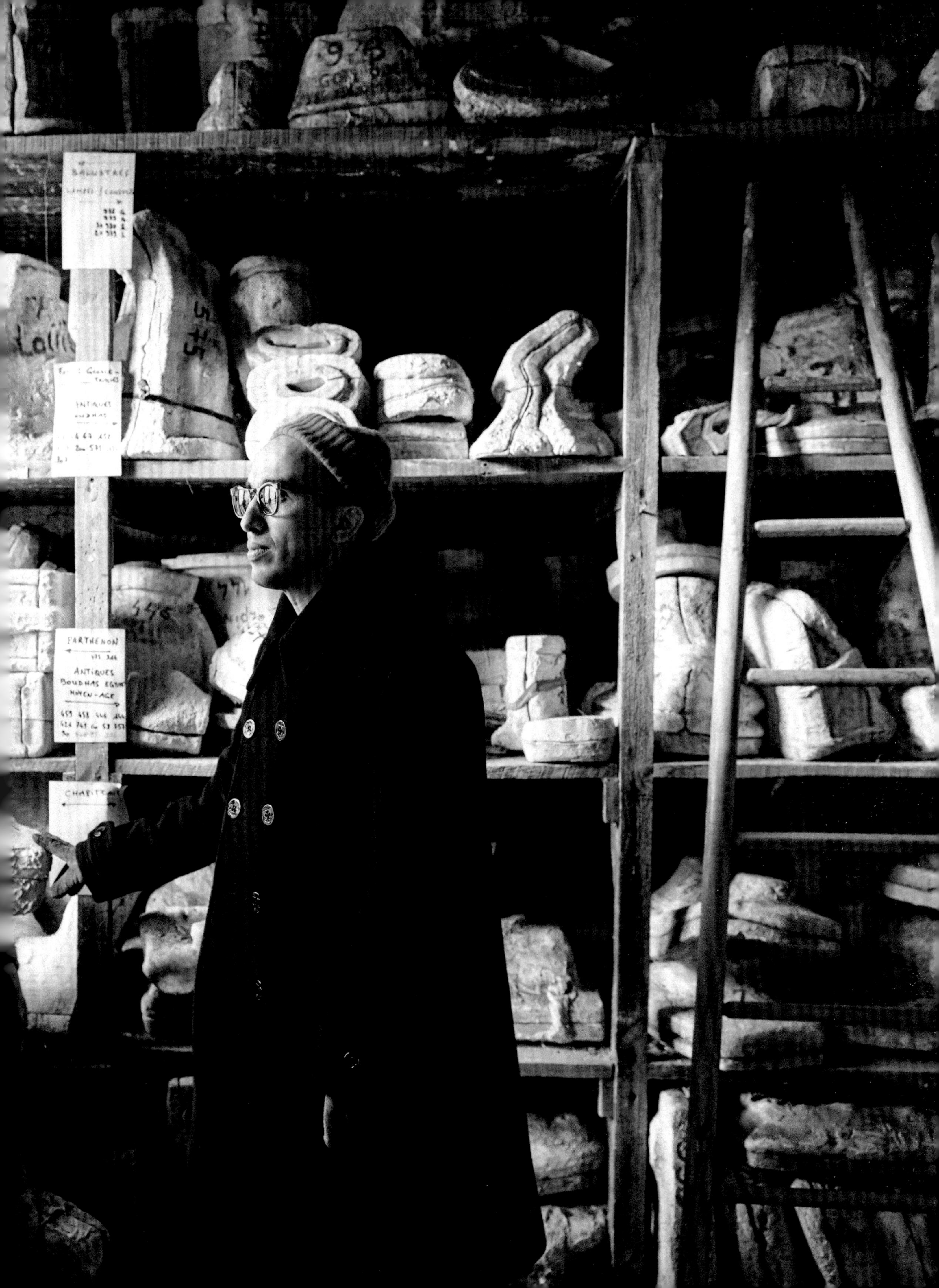
BALUSTRES
PARTHENON
ANTIQUES
MOYEN-AGE

Ramdane Touhami doesn't dominate the room the way some entrepreneurs do. He is casually dressed in comfortable trousers, sneakers and a warm-looking wooly sweater and hat. It is a contrast from the smart smock-like navy jackets worn by the staff at his Parisian beauty emporium, Officine Universelle Buly. Touhami, 42, seems a sprightly, nimble man who, one suspects, could quickly take you down in a boxing match. Certainly, through the refined spaces he is creating, he is hitting it big in the rarified world of premium cosmetics.

On the horizon is a new store in London (a 400-square-foot boutique in Selfridges), with locations in Milan and Los Angeles to follow. Touhami has launched an almost meteoric brand expansion; these new projects will join the 14 other outposts that have opened within just three years of operations. Can he divulge any details? "Erm, *non*," he replies, a little tersely. "I prefer to speak about things when they are done."

Each store has its own unique identity; from New York to Hong Kong, interior intricacies impart a mood or theme. At the store here in the Marais, for example, there's a rectangular cast-iron framed pit, cut into the floorboards. Touhami gestures, "See that? That's where Rodin cast his *Thinker*." Indeed, we are in the workshop where the Parisian sculptor created his celebrated seated figure. For Touhami, who designs each space himself, paying attention to historical detail is almost an obsession. The more time that is spent with him, the more it becomes apparent that he too is something of a thinker. Far from the brooding, deeply pensive type immortalized by Rodin, however, this fashion designer, brand creator, businessman and occasional DJ is a man of action.

"I'm selling a fantasy image of Paris to the world," he replies when asked to describe the Buly concept. It is a meticulously curated universe grounded in what he considers the heyday of retail: the 19th century, when, under the rule of Napoleon, the production and trading of crafted commodities became a Parisian specialty. In fact, the 700 products in Buly's cosmetics range were inspired by 19th-century French apothecaries. Touhami revels in talking about the history of retail and likes to go into great detail when describing the Paris that once was—how Rue Saint-Honoré was perhaps the world's first "luxury street," and how Le Bon Marché invented the department store. "It was a golden era," he says, his face animated.

Touhami's own vision of luxury is based on a deep respect for quality. It embodies what used to be called *recherché*, in which all is researched and carefully realized. But the atmosphere at Buly is light years away from the stuffy, spotless luxury that often dominates the market. *Luxury*, in fact, is a word that Touhami loathes; the mere mention provokes spitting profanities. "This is not luxury!" he argues, using plenty of expletives to describe what he sees elsewhere as an uninspired and inflated industry. (He is no less scathing about the "boring people" who run some of Paris' most famous houses by focusing on spreadsheets and margins.)

Indeed, Touhami is ardently unorthodox and happy to cultivate an outsider persona. He was raised in a Moroccan-French family in the countryside before dropping out of school at 17 to create Teuchiland, a T-shirt brand which parodied Timberland with a reference to cannabis. At the age of 18, he found himself on the wrong side of a Toulouse gang and escaped to Paris where, penniless, he lived on the streets for a year, seeking shelter in metro stations, under bridges and in public bathrooms. He was stabbed and bears the scar to this day.

Touhami requires that his staff be versed in calligraphy, to better prepare hand-written gift labels, price tags and book dedications. Those who don't manage to master the art? "They're fired!" Touhami jokes.

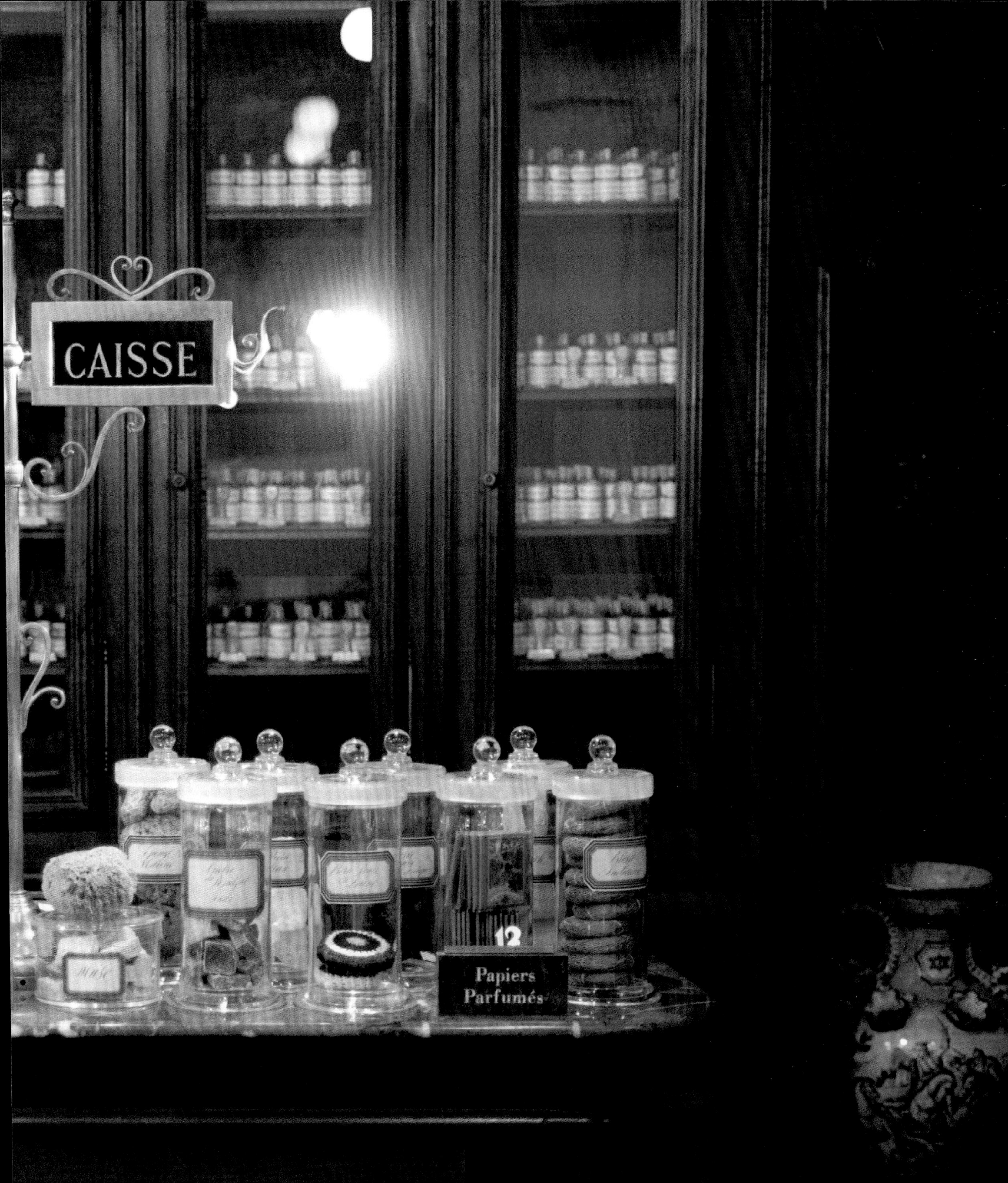
CAISSE
12
Papiers
Parfumés

Gradually, Touhami left the streets and created various streetwear and skateboarding brands. He began to build up his career with more business-focused ventures including L'Épicerie, a concept store he founded with designers Marc Jacobs and Jeremy Scott in 1998. He also hosted a television show called *Strip-Tease*, owned a donkey polo club in Tangier and spent time in Tokyo rebuilding fashion retail brand And A. He was menswear director at Liberty London and, in 2007, was in charge of revamping opulent Parisian candlemaker Maison de Cire Trudon.

Though the path from Liberty and Cire Trudon to Buly seems to show his progression toward historic brands, Touhami protests that his early career is not incongruous with what he is creating at present. "It's the same," he insists. "There's a big connection between my skate brand and what I do now... My slogan was 'French Savoir Faire.' We created our own French style with a twist." And that certainly seems to describe what Touhami is still doing today—albeit with the florid veneer of the belle epoque in his toolbox.

Although scornful of big luxury stores, he praises fresher, more urban retail brands such as Aesop. Touhami may flit from one subject to the next with sometimes confusing rapidity, but he is always refreshingly lucid about his modus operandi: "Those big brands make all their stores look exactly the same," he says. "Then, there are brands like Aesop that ask local designers to come up with a new concept for each location. And then there's me—I design everything myself. It's a bit extreme. This is not a democratic company, *eh*!" As well as a vision of Paris, Touhami is either knowingly or unknowingly exporting himself.

His hyper-personal approach is clear when walking through the different spaces, rooms and back offices of the labyrinthine shop and workshop in the Marais. In one room, a row of five people are working at spotlit desks. Here, Buly's chief calligrapher, Paul, teaches his craft to all of the retail assistants. Everyone is expected to do four hours of calligraphy a week to reach the exacting standards required to write personalized gift labels and book dedications, as well as notices and price tags. Asked why he invests so much time in such a seemingly minor task, Touhami responds: "I think in only one generation people will not know how to write by hand." What if the staff doesn't manage to execute such beautiful cursive? "They are fired!" Touhami says, perhaps only half-joking.

Like fine handwriting, the art of wrapping packages is a celebrated art at Officine Universelle Buly. Its "head wrapper" has mastered over 600 varieties of folds.

"*I design everything myself. It's a bit extreme. This is not a democratic company.*"

Another essential component of the Buly experience is gift wrapping. Buly's head wrapper was trained personally by the only surviving family that practices Japanese *origata*—an exponentially more complex craft than origami that was traditionally reserved to service the paper-folding needs of the imperial court. There are some 3,600 different folds in origata; so far Touhami's colleague has managed "only" 600 different pleats. Again, Touhami shows his love for specialized craft—the smaller and more niche, the better. "Origata is like a language—an aristocratic, Japanese language," he says.

Touhami may seem to be one of a kind, but he doesn't do it all alone. He collaborates with his wife, Victoire De Taillac, on developing and sustaining the brand. Their latest project is *An Atlas of Natural Beauty: Botanical Ingredients for Retaining and Enhancing Beauty*, a beautifully bound book featuring illustrations of plants and extracts, informative texts, historical anecdotes and related proverbs. From the almost miraculous properties of the lotus flower to the astringent, purifying powers of geranium, it's a fascinating read even for those with little interest in skincare.

Constantly (but politely) fielding phone calls, including one from his boxing instructor, Touhami operates at a frenetic pace. Is boxing a way to relax, one wonders? "It's a way to avoid killing someone!" he jokes, explaining some of the frustrations that come with success. "It's more about speed. When you have so many things to do, you wish that other people were moving at your speed too." With his Buly empire staffed by almost 100 people and shops sprouting the world over, it is becoming an increasingly difficult operation to micromanage. But it is obvious that Touhami would not (and probably could not) have it any other way. When he ponders how it might be to work with him, he's self-aware: "My God, I am the worst!"

Touhami embodies all the bravado and banter of somebody who is both supremely confident and ambitious. When asked how it feels to be unrivaled in his influence on the Parisian retail scene, he scoffs: "Paris is just a village! It's nothing." The energetic creator and designer explains how the success of the business depends on the happiness of everyone involved, from his employees to the makers of the products—even to himself. Finally, he says, "The best is when the customer is happy and they think nobody screwed them over. When they agree the price is reasonable and the product is good." He makes it sound simple, but Touhami's constant quest for the highest quality is clearly hard work. His efforts, however, are putting the Buly name firmly in the history of Parisian shopping.

Boxing is Touhami's way of working stress out of his system. His boxing coach was France's champion fighter seven times over, Touhami says.

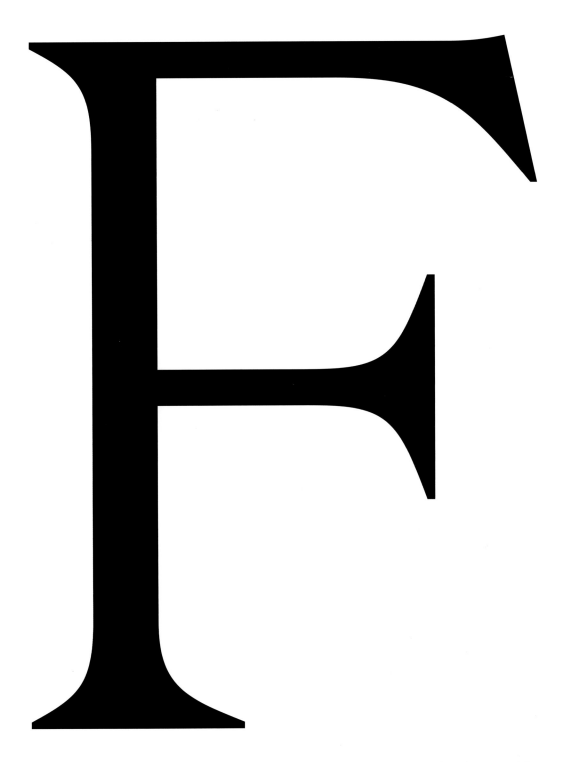

rance's musical revolution had a start date: June 22, 1963. That was the day that, to celebrate the first anniversary of the magazine Salut les copains (literally "Hello buddies!"), the journal's parent radio station, Europe 1, organized a free concert in Paris' Place de la Nation. The line-up of Johnny Hallyday, Sylvie Vartan and Richard Anthony attracted 150,000 revelers. Some danced on rooftops. Others watched the spectacle from the treetops of the nearby Bois de Vincennes park as they puffed Disque Bleu cigarettes (for the aspirational woman) or the filterless Gauloises beloved of Serge Gainsbourg (for male artistes)…

Words by Tristan Rutherford

The following day, *Paris-Presse* screamed the headline *Salut les voyous!* ("Hello Hooligans!"). Other journals deplored the perceived violence of the *blousons noirs*, the work-averse ruffians in black leather jackets inspired by James Dean in *Rebel Without a Cause*. Writing in *Le Monde*, sociologist Edgar Morin baptized them *yé-yés* after The Beatles' lyrics from "She Loves You." Even French President Charles de Gaulle chimed in: "These youngsters seem to have so much energy to spend. Let's have them build roads." Since the seeds of French pop had been sown during France's baby boom two decades earlier, the *Salut les copains* generation was the first in living memory never to have experienced war directly. There was hope and promise in the Paris summer air.

As a young girl from Paris' 16th Arrondissement, Françoise Hardy listened to mainstream rockers Cliff Richard and The Everly Brothers on pirate station Radio Luxembourg. She was painfully shy and woefully naïve—an anti-Bardot who didn't wear lipstick or smoke. Her father's greatest contribution was to gift her a guitar for passing her *baccalauréat*. After answering a newspaper advertisement from record label Disques Vogue calling for young singers, she found herself in a downtown studio in 1962 at the age of 18. She laid down the track "Tous les garçons et les filles" "in three hours with the worst four musicians in Paris."

The vinyl spun on Europe 1 during the station's original *Salut les copains* radio slot, a daily show increasingly dedicated to Yé-Yé. Hardy's singsong intonation carried a naïf allure. High notes haunt while melodies are timeless. Handwritten lyrics speak of a "happy heart without fear of tomorrow." The photo of the doe-eyed teen that peeps from the vinyl cover sleeve matches the lyrics. It portrays a naturalness that could have been culled from her high school yearbook.

Hardy's first hit song, "Tous les garçons et les filles", sold 700,000 copies in France and was recorded in French, English, Italian and German.

Throughout her career Hardy has been notoriously shy, which she often attributes in interviews to her astrological sign, Capricorn.

Hardy was France embodied: poised, invigorated and born into an era of new hope. By the following year, the song had sold a million copies and was awarded a gold disc. It was covered in a dozen languages from Swedish to Vietnamese and spearheaded a Yé-Yé movement that would storm the 1960s. From timidity and diffidence, a star was born.

In 1963, when Hardy turned 19, her peers were on the cusp of a revolution. It was the year that chanteuse Édith Piaf and her fellow Parisian friend Jean Cocteau passed away. In their place were born shoe designer Christian Louboutin and porn star Lolo Ferrari, later symbols of a modern, sexy and more outrageous France. Within another year, people under 21 would make up a third of the French population. And the average adolescent's disposable income was a whopping 122 francs per week.

The nation itself was in the midst of *Les Trente Glorieuses*. During this 30-year period, from 1945 to 1975, the French economy grew at a breakneck four percent per annum. Salaries rose by 200 percent until Parisians—if not their rural compatriots—could declare themselves amongst the richest in the world. When "Tous les garçons et les filles" was released, one quarter of French families owned a television and could watch the track's dodgy pop video produced for Scopitone, a 16mm format originally made for French "film jukeboxes." Four years later, in 1966, half of France possessed a TV set.

The Place de la Nation concert in Paris was shot for *Salut les copains* magazine by Jean-Marie Périer. It was an era where journalists and photographers could mix freely with stars such as Hardy and Hallyday. They could sip pastis and grenadine *tomates* at Régine or Chez Castel with singer France Gall and model Anita Pallenberg. Or bag kaftans at vintage stores like Mamie Blue on rue de Rochechouart. (Paris being a *ville-musée*, all three timeless institutions still exist.) Périer originally trained his lens on the love affair between Yé-Yé's star couple, Johnny Hallyday and Sylvie Vartan. But after setting his camera on Hardy, four years his junior, Périer was struck by her magnetism. Love blossomed as her record sales approached one million. In his photos, he presented her as the quintessential girl next door. Subsequent album covers from *Le premier bonheur du jour* positioned Hardy as a shyly smiling teen dressed in a knitted jersey of which her grandmother would have approved. The following year, Disques Vogue released her 1964 album, *Mon amie la rose*, and Périer's cover image highlights Hardy's timid profile. Only her EP for *l'Amitié*, released the following year, shows any whisper of French sass coupled with the barest sliver of midriff, which just hints at the sexier Latin-quarter styles of Saint-Germain.

In this era of Yuri Gagarin and Jacques Cousteau, Périer also dressed his lover as both an astronaut and an ocean princess. Back in 1965, record producers and label executives were exclusively male; their female protégés were marionettes in a patriarchal world. Elsa Leroy was discovered in a beauty contest, and Kiki Caron had been a swimming champion.

> *"Hardy was France embodied: poised, invigorated and born into an era of new hope."*

As Hardy herself admitted: "If I'd been four feet tall and 15 stone, I would certainly not have followed the same career."

But during the mid-1960s, social barriers were demolished quicker than the *bidonvilles*, the migrant slums for Italian, Portuguese and Algerian workers flattened to make way for roads and trains. As these suburban links were constructed, 22-year-old entrepreneur James Arch came up with a system to bus partygoers into central Paris for two francs. In 1965, his aptly named Bus Palladium opened on rue Fontaine in the 9th Arrondissement as a place for young men and women to flirt, rock and dance *le jerk*. "Everything happened at the same time," says Jean-Emmanuel Deluxe, whose book *Yé-Yé Girls of '60s French Pop* captures the period. "Women's liberation, Godard's *Masculin Féminin*, a new openness about sexuality."

Bus Palladium's no-dress code rule was the antithesis of Régine and Chez Castel—and an imme-

Jacques Dutronc and Françoise Hardy
began their relationship in 1967, had
a son together in 1973, and were
married in 1981—"for tax reasons,"
says Hardy.

diate success. Arch leafleted moviegoers lining up for the Beatles' film *Help!*, and they rushed in after the movie's credits. Inside, Hallyday played, Mick Jagger celebrated his birthday, and Salvador Dalí dropped in with an entourage and drank only Vittel water. Hardy's full album release of *l'Amitié* showed the 21-year-old's sultry smolder on the sleeve cover—a Parisian sophisticate staring in the distance. "Françoise Hardy's rise was independent," explains Deluxe. "She was the first star to author her own lyrics, to write her own music. Some other female singers were puppets in a male dominated industry, but her no longer."

The dawn of globalization brought increasing notoriety. In 1965—a year of assassinations, coups and escalating war—Hardy rereleased *Dans le monde entier* in English as *All Over the World*. Each international release had its own title to chime with local sensibilities: *Françoise Hardy Sings* in Canada; *Françoise Hardy Sings in English* for suspicious South Africans; and *The "Yeh-Yeh" Girl From Paris!* for American listeners who required more explanation. "Yé-Yé didn't copy British or American rock and roll," says Deluxe. "It was not a mere cover. It has riskier lyrics, plus jazzier French rhythms infused with European verve." Bob Dylan dedicated a poem to Hardy. The Beatles dreamt of dating her. Périer shot a portrait of Jagger alongside his "ideal woman"—the Rolling Stone looking sly and proprietorial, the French singer appearing elegantly disinterested, as well as an inch taller.

Middle America took note. In a 1964 issue of *LIFE*, where the cover story featured Jacqueline Kennedy's reminiscences on her late husband, "Hooray for the Yé-Yé Girls" explained, "What the Beatles are to England, the singing Yé-Yé girls are to France." Between advertisements for the Kodak Instam-atic Camera and Twist's Instant Lemonade, the magazine nailed Hardy's profile. "She not only sings but also composes her own music. A dreamy contemplative sort… tall, intellectual and very good-looking. Says Françoise: 'I can't stand to wear anything that will make people look at me.'" France was sexier than thou and foreign musicians scrabbled for walk-on parts; Gainsbourg penned French songs, for release in France, for Petula Clark and Marianne Faithfull.

The green metal newsstands dotted around Paris perpetuated the Yé-Yé myth. At the age of 19, Périer's half-sister Anne-Marie became editor-in-chief of *Mademoiselle Âge Tendre* (literally "Miss Young Lady"), a teenage offshoot of *Salut les copains*. It struck a blow for feminism by being staffed entirely by young women. The letters editor, Anne Braillard, was just 16. Hardy typically graced the cover. Stories inside covered the lives of Catherine Deneuve and Alain Delon, or *Les vacances sportives de Sylvie et Johnny*. Star tips on dating, knitting and holiday plans embodied girlish innocence and boundless positivity. In year one, monthly readership topped 400,000.

Hardy followed the dating tips she penned for *Mademoiselle Âge Tendre*. In 1966, the rising star at Disques Vogue was Jacques Dutronc, whose jerking Jagger-style bop to *J'ai Mis Un Tigre Dans Ma Guitare* ("I put a tiger in my guitar") sold 300,000 copies. *Salut les copains* lapped up the male soloist, who fell for Hardy, his label mate, the following year. The inaugural edition of *Special Pop* claimed of Hardy: "More than a singer, she's becoming a universal myth with whom thousands of young girls dream of identifying." Dutronc evidently thought the same.

Alas, their rock-star relationship was perhaps typical. Even following the birth of their son,

> "She was the first star to author her own lyrics, to write her own music. Some other female singers were puppets in a male dominated industry, but her no longer."

Hardy vowed to retire from the music industry before she reached 50. Today, at age 75, her legacy as a seminal musician and style icon of 1960s Paris lives on.

> *"More than a singer, she's a universal myth with whom thousands of girls dream of identifying."*

Thomas Dutronc, in 1973, Jacques took a year to settle with them, after a brief affair with the French-German actress Romy Schneider. "He set me up for an appointment, twice a month," Hardy remembers. In her latest book, *A Gift of Heaven*, she claims to still feel "tenderness" for Dutronc, whom she married in 1981. "I think it's mutual. And when you have lived the best years of your life with someone, it creates a link." Still married, they live in separate homes today.

Yé-Yé floundered too. After the Summer of Love came the Prague Spring and Vietnam demonstrations of 1968. Pop music sold out, became high on drugs or traveled to India for spiritual succor. In May 1968, an out-of-touch Charles de Gaulle was confronted by two weeks of strikes from the Sorbonne University to the Renault factory in Boulogne-Billancourt and a month of protests. Jean-Paul Sartre manned barricades of paving slabs pulled up to halt the riot police. "*Sous les pavés, la plage!*" ("Under the cobblestones, the beach!"). Hardy and Dutronc fled from Paris to Corsica to escape the violence. The demonstrations ended when trade unions accepted a 35 percent increase in the minimum wage and de Gaulle called for new parliamentary elections.

Through the 1970s, the girl next door cut a worldly figure. Hardy left the male-dominated world of Disques Vogue to start her own record firm. Her label's second album release, *La question*, addressed her instabilities with Dutronc and is considered peerless, if not exactly pop music. The introvert from the 16th eventually released nearly 30 studio albums. And her global Yé-Yé movement inspired Japan's Shibuya-kei kitsch pop, collaborations with Blur and, arguably, a 14-year-old songstress named Vanessa Paradis. The dancing kiss in the Wes Anderson film *Moonrise Kingdom* could only be set to Hardy's music—in this instance "Le temps de l'amour." And just as restless as she was 55 years ago, Hardy is penning a new album for 2018 release. In her own words: "I never get bored. There isn't enough time in the day."

In the annals of French music, Jacques Dutronc is often grouped with iconic songwriter Serge Gainsbourg. Critic Alexandra Marshall recently described them as "intellectuals who sang from the head, even when their lyrical content was perverse."

HARRIET FITCH LITTLE

Recently Deleted

How technology is changing our memories of family.

It's been three years since my mom stopped using her camera. "It's just easier," she said, announcing our first smartphone-documented Christmas. "I can email the pictures to your uncle in Spain." Then, with the patience of someone reasoning with a Luddite, "You know, I can always print them off later." Of course, I understood, having myself lost patience with everything not instantly shareable a long time before my parents capitulated to the cheap thrills of click and send. But, selfishly, it felt like a loss. The role of family photographer is a bit like that of designated driver—I don't want to do it, but I certainly want *someone* to be behind the wheel.

Photo albums are a historic ledger of sorts: They celebrate the living, memorialize the dead, and knit your life together with those of others in neat chronological order. It's oddly grounding. The photographer Erik Kessels, who has trawled through thousands of abandoned family albums for his found photography project *In Almost Every Picture*, has identified eight albums created by the typical family. The first has shots of the courting couple, with each subsequent album charting the addition of a child or grandchild to the clan.

In digital space, these timelines become hazy. Family life is now chronicled in the media folders of a dozen different WhatsApp conversations, and in Facebook albums that some of those pictured can't even access. There is no single repository, no consistent curation. Each platform has its own life span, none of them infinite. And the transition from physical to digital photography has changed how we think about the function of images. This is the argument of Silke Arnold-de Simine—a cultural theorist who co-edited the anthology *Picturing the Family*, published in February 2018. "[Online], a photograph connects us to friends and family who are not here at the moment. It is to say, 'Look what I'm doing now,' rather than any form of remembering," she says. So, in colloquial terms, pictures of my family's Christmas dinner are no longer being taken for the sake of posterity, but to be whizzed around the world to those who can't be at the table.

Academics are rarely nostalgic, and Arnold-de Simine thinks there are logical reasons why we now use photos to "connect us in space rather than time": We live farther apart, and our lives are so abundantly documented that the idea of needing glue-and-stick images to remember them feels faintly ridiculous.

And yet personally I feel the pangs of loss. Partly it's that the physical family album is such a resoundingly solid statement of belonging—a totem that has its origins in the Victorian family home. Partly it's that since we stopped printing photos we've forgotten that snapshot moments are worth preserving.

My family albums are bursting with poorly composed pictures of unimportant moments—my aunt cooking in a steamed-up kitchen, toddlers in wading pools, half-baked attempts at costumes. Many of these images have become privately iconic: The best photo ever taken of me is a casual snap of me breastfeeding as a baby, the look of bliss on my chubby face so pure that I have enlarged the photo and hung it in my kitchen. Now, these in-the-moment images are captured on phones and most often stay there. Last autumn, I came across *Milky Way*—a series of snapshots that the high-art photographer Vincent Ferrané had taken of his wife breastfeeding. In one image she's almost asleep, in another she's on the phone. These are photographs of the quiet, incidental moments that beat out the rhythm of day-to-day life. *Milky Way* has been widely celebrated, and rightly so—the images are loving and quietly revealing. But let's not abandon the family album to the professionals. This is a field that is, by its very definition, wide open to amateurs. Thanks to my parents, I have my own approximation of a Ferrané hanging on my kitchen wall. And if we want to pass on similar snapshots to our children, we'll have to start treating click-and-send photos like they matter.

In Silke Arnold-de Simine's recent publication, *Picturing the Family*, a roster of academics use different photographs as case studies to understand how families perceive memory and identity collectively.

Under Your Nose

Gorillas in the midst, and what else we miss when we're not looking.

Picture this: You step into the subway, settle into a seat and begin scrolling through emails, articles and notifications on your phone. When you look up, you realize you've missed your stop. Essentially, the activities happening on your little screen consumed so much attention that you became oblivious to your surroundings. Experiences like this happen all the time and reveal how we can miss obvious, often important, things that are right in front of us.

Perhaps the best-known example of this is an experiment by psychologists Christopher Chabris and Daniel Simons, published in 1999. Subjects were asked to watch a video in which six basketball players in white and black T-shirts passed around a ball. They were instructed to count the number of passes made by those wearing white. At one point, a woman in a gorilla suit walks through the players, faces the camera and thumps her chest before sauntering off the court. Surprisingly, half of the viewers who participated in the experiment failed to notice the gorilla.

"People seem to have the intuitive belief that they will notice unexpected things that cross their line of sight," says Chabris, who, with Simons, co-authored *The Invisible Gorilla: And Other Ways Our Intuition Deceives Us,* a book that delves into the everyday implications of their study. "We found that people can completely fail to notice very salient objects right in front of their eyes if they're paying attention to something else."

This psychological phenomenon is known as "inattentional blindness" and it helps explain why we miss blatant bloopers in a film or bump into people in front of us when texting-while-walking. However, being aware of the limits of our attention is a good first step in noticing the goings on around us. If we're looking to improve our skills in this area, a good starting point is to at least be aware of our tendency to get wrapped up in one thing at a time.

KEYED IN

by Charmaine Li

You were sure you left your keys in your coat pocket, but now they seem to have disappeared. Even though misplacing objects is a common occurrence, it's still a frustrating (and time-consuming) experience. Small items that are used often, like keys, get lost more easily because it's less likely you're paying full attention each time you set them down. Typically, a search involves returning to places where you expect objects to be, when in fact they've been left in a location you don't usually put them. "You can even look at the place where your keys are and not notice them, because you don't expect them to be there," says psychologist Christopher Chabris. How does he recommend combatting everyday forgetfulness? Do one thing at a time to avoid burdening your attention.

Photograph: Noell Oszvald

MATT CASTLE

Finding Francis

For talented people to share and use their gifts to full advantage, somebody first needs to ferret them out. In 1879, a Manchester-based medical student and aspiring writer named Francis Thompson received a copy of Thomas De Quincey's memoir, *Confessions of an English Opium-Eater*, from his mother. De Quincey's flowery descriptions of the pleasures and pains of opium stirred Thompson's unease at the prospect of a medical career and nudged him toward a different path. Already unwell with what was probably his first bout of tuberculosis, Thompson started taking opium himself both for symptom relief and for literary inspiration.

After failing his final examinations, he abandoned his studies to seek his fortune in London as a poet. But his deepening drug addiction triggered a steady descent into destitution. Short-lived jobs as an assistant in a boot shop, a newspaper seller and a matchstick vendor petered out. Thompson's literary ambitions were dealt a blow when libraries refused him entrance due to his unkempt appearance. Soon he was reduced to sleeping rough under the arches of Covent Garden.

Throughout this desperate time, he wrote. His pockets were stuffed with scraps of paper inscribed with verse. His style was distinctive: He tended to use obscure or self-coined words and unusual punctuation, parentheses and turns of phrase. His themes were often mystical or spiritual—his parents were Catholic converts, and Thompson had considered the priesthood before starting his medical studies. But the language and imagery of his work were deeply colored by his experiences of poverty and addiction.

In February 1887, he pushed an essay and some poems penned on scruffy paper through the door of the offices of the magazine *Merry England*, with the following postscript: "Please address your rejection to the Charing Cross Post Office." It took six months for Wilfrid and Alice Meynell, the husband-and-wife team who edited the journal, to properly examine the scribblings. Immediately, they recognized an unusual talent, and took to the streets of London in search of Thompson. Eventually, they tracked down and "saved" him—initially feeding and lodging him in their own home, and at last providing him with an outlet for his writing. Although he didn't find great fame in his lifetime, he went on to publish a handful of critically acclaimed poetry volumes. Later figures inspired by his work include G.K. Chesterton and J.R.R. Tolkien. But Francis Thompson's rescue was only ever a partial success. Over time, his life drifted back toward disorder, characterized by bouts of ill health, opium use and frequent moves between lodging houses, monastic retreats and the homes of well-meaning patrons. While the Meynells demonstrated a clear sense of responsibility toward the talent they had uncovered and nurtured—something not always apparent in contemporary tales of discovery and sudden success—Thompson remained set on a tragic trajectory. He died at the age of 47, ruined by the deadly combination of Mycobacterium tuberculosis and opiate addiction.

PIP USHER

Cult Rooms

Beloved Lower East Side institution Russ & Daughters has spent the past 103 years perfecting the art of "appetizing." The term encompasses the many delicacies associated with that ultimate Jewish-American culinary tradition—the bagel. From wafer-thin slices of smoked salmon to delicate curls of red onion and handfuls of juicy capers, this neon-lit establishment serves New York City's finest selection of smoked fish, pickled herring fillets and cream cheese spreads on freshly baked bagels.

When founder Joel Russ arrived in America at the turn of the 20th century, he made his living peddling schmaltz herring from a pushcart to his fellow Eastern European Jews. A brick and mortar store, Russ, eventually opened on East Houston Street. Three daughters later, the shop's name changed. A century on, Russ & Daughters is a renowned purveyor of Jewish-American food to a devoted following. Throughout the many changes, the store's pursuit of perfection has remained.

"It's meditative, in a way," says fourth-generation co-owner Josh Russ Tupper as he cleaves smoothly through a hunk of smoked salmon. Clad in a white chef's coat, he is being filmed for another of the city's revered establishments, *The New Yorker*, to celebrate the store's centennial. "It's always different," he adds. "You know, I'm going to cut a half pound of salmon, the shape of the slices are going to change entirely as I do that, and I'm constantly reevaluating the fish as I slice."

"The strokes are very subtle," chimes in another salmon-carving maestro behind the counter, who boasts a trim mustache and elegantly arched eyebrows. "The movements should be as if you were playing the violin, right, very gently, and your eyes go back and forth." Such craftsmanship—coupled with the store's deeply nostalgic decor—has cemented its standing on New York's culinary scene. And, in 2015, the opening of a Russ & Daughters café in the Jewish Museum suggested an even more profound legacy; those barrels of salty herring that Russ hawked around his neighborhood's poverty-stricken streets are now an emblem of Jewish pride in the city.

But back to the salmon: "Then you come up with a slice that you can see through," concludes the man with the mustache as he holds up a translucent sliver of silky fish. The message is clear: any old schmuck can fillet a fish, but at Russ & Daughters, slicing salmon remains an art form.

For those unable to visit, *Russ & Daughters: Reflections and Recipes From the House That Herring Built* is a cookbook offering insight into the store's lore and legend from the grandson of its founder.

Previous page: Photograph by Alexander Rotondo, Left photograph: Plasa

PETER SMISEK

Momčilo Milovanović

Totemic is the first word that comes to mind when contemplating the oeuvre of the late Serbian sculptor Momčilo Milovanović. This impression, instantaneous as it may be, is anything but superficial, and Milovanović's extraordinary life provides vital clues to the genius of his often towering works.

Milovanović was born in 1921 in the small town of Smederevska Palanka in eastern Serbia, then part of Yugoslavia. Although the town wasn't far from the capital, Belgrade, Milovanović spent his youth in the countryside, where he developed the relationship with nature that would have a profound effect on his later work. As a teenager, he moved to Belgrade with his father and uncles, helping out with the family business after having dropped out of secondary school. In 1941, Yugoslavia was invaded and quickly fell under Nazi control; by 1943, Milovanović had escaped to Vienna to avoid forced labor and, at the behest of an acquaintance, enrolled at the Academy of Fine Arts Vienna. Later that year, he was arrested while trying to visit Munich's Pinakothek art museum. He managed to escape from prison one year later, returning to Belgrade to join the army

just as the Second World War drew to a close. Finally, in 1950, after a decade of displacement, he enrolled in Belgrade's Academy of Fine Arts at the age of 28.

At the time, artistic training in Yugoslavia was still grounded in figurative representation, and Milovanović received a thoroughly classical training while financing his studies by working as a manual laborer. His work from this period betrays a somewhat stifling, academic influence, but he also began working with scraps of wood and metal—a testament to a life of struggle and hard work.

In 1960, after obtaining his specialization in sculpture, Milovanović traveled to Paris with nothing but 50 francs in his pocket. There, he discovered abstraction in sculpture through the work of Constantin Brâncuși and began to experiment with this new style, oscillating between figuration and abstraction throughout the next decade. Some of his bronzes, such as the elegantly polished *Oeuf Cassé*, betray Brâncuși's influence, but the visual weight, symmetry and sense of reverence given to the object hint at Milovanović's developing formal idiom. *Torse de Jeune Homme*, one of

his smaller works from the same period, takes on a refined, asymmetrical and almost Hellenistic form. But it is wood's irregular and coarse grain that was to become the sculptor's trademark. While refining his sculpture, he continued producing small paintings on discarded wood during this period, which he sold to make a living.

It did not take long for Milovanović to gain acclaim: During his first exhibition in 1961 at the Galerie des Jeunes, his work was noticed by art critic Denys Chevalier, who brought him to the attention of the French Minister of Culture.

An artistic breakthrough came in 1970 when Milovanović returned to abstraction for good. The following two decades marked a period of prodigious activity for the sculptor and produced a coherent output. Although he employed a range of materials— wood, marble, concrete, steel, aluminum, copper and bronze—the sculptures became more robust, more rhythmically textured, and more totemic. The veins in marble and the cracks in wood are used to give an almost primal, earthy quality to his more mature works. The totems vary in size, some small and precious, others sublime and

monumental, commissioned to give a strong sense of place and identity, often to public spaces.

"Milovanović is a doyen and one of the most important contemporary artists in Serbian sculpture," says Paris-based Serbian-born artist and critic Milija Belić, who helped organize a retrospective of Milovanović's work in Belgrade in 2010. "Although reduced and simple, these fundamental geometric works are laden with archetypal meanings."

There is a strong naturalist streak in Milovanović's work, as well as a nod to folklore. This latter notion, says Belić, should be understood in the context of Victor Vasarely's *Planetary Folklore*, a series of compositions in which the artist used a limited number of visual components. Illustrating this point, he points to a likely formal idiom in Vasarely and Milovanović's shared motherland: medieval stećak stones. Thousands of these carved and solemn stone grave-markers are dotted around the Bosnian, Serbian and Croatian countryside. Like Milovanović's totems, they reflect a compromise between the universal and the highly personal, and between the human and the sacred.

In 1978, Milovanović moved to Mantes-La-Ville in the western suburbs of Paris, where he lived and worked until his death in 2013.

Some translation required: Starred clues reveal common English words borrowed from French.

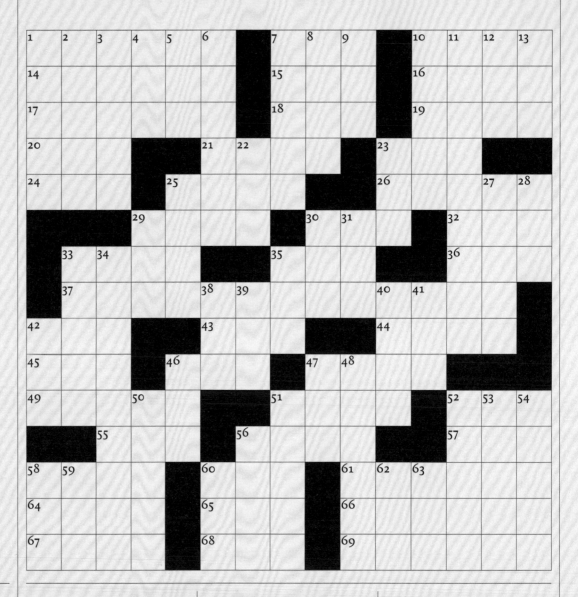

Crossword

ACROSS

1. *Banality
7. Excavated
10. *Stylish
14. ____ balloon
15. Finish
16. Repetitive learning technique
17. Schedule
18. Protagonist of Dickens' "Great Expectations"
19. Approximately
20. Perimeter
21. Place to insert a coin
23. Helpful connections
24. Rappers
25. Rendezvous
26. Worm once used by ancient Greek physicians
29. Earth, Wind & ____
30. Nocturnal bird of prey
32. Sheep's cry
33. Prayer conclusion
35. Arthur Miller play "Death ___ Salesman"
36. Perform in a play, say
37. How to solve the starred clues
42. Scrap
43. Poem of praise
44. Stirred from sleep
45. Cozy lodge
46. Sound of disapproval from an audience
47. Key ingredient in borscht
49. Milk farm
51. Dwellers on Mount Olympus, in Greek myth
52. Master
55. Stocking stuffer?
56. Mythical Himalayan creature
57. Fluffy feather accessory
58. *Stroke
60. Number of fingers humans have
61. Pulses
64. *Assistant
65. Serving of corn
66. *Body of work
67. Ran in the laundry
68. Exist
69. Unmask

DOWN

1. Enchant
2. Sound reasoning
3. Listings on a menu
4. Avant-garde band with the 1971 album "Tago Mago"
5. Concealed
6. Pencil topper
7. *Drop-off point for a train
8. Apartment, for example
9. Measure of a country's economic performance
10. Witchy figure in fairytales
11. Type of riding
12. "___ a Wonderful Life"
13. Corporate fig.
22. Film Director Spike
23. 1986 Beastie Boys album "Licensed to ___"
25. Short skirt
27. *Hiding place
28. Fedora, for example
29. Comedian and writer Tina
30. Askew
31. Armed conflict
33. Yoga position
34. Importance
35. The loneliest number
38. Also
39. Wedding words
40. Mother sheep
41. "To be or ___ to be"
42. Remove
46. "Ciao!"
47. Likely producer of email spam
48. Member of a film crew or magazine staff
50. Lassoed
51. *Type
52. Over
53. Lethal hooded snake
54. Painter's stand
56. Joan Didion's "The ___ of Magical Thinking"
58. Taxi
59. Corn or soybean product
60. Drink served with scones and clotted cream
62. Color
63. Gun the engine

Djassi DaCosta Johnson

In her interview with Michaela DePrince on page 92, writer Djassi DaCosta Johnson, herself a dancer, finds a role model among a younger generation.

Illustration: Chidy Wayne

It was a wonderful revelation to find in Michaela an intelligent and thoughtful dancer who is cognizant of the world around her, and her place in it. I have often felt that dancers have been infantilized; the status quo of being "seen and not heard" is maintained to suit the institution, company or environment in which the dancer is immersed. It is important to note a marked shift from the nameless and voiceless dancer whose job it was simply to look beautiful, be technically excellent and transform themselves into a character, real or fantastical. The intelligence of many dancers has long been undermined, and interviewing Michaela was a wonderful affirmation that times are changing and the most gorgeous and influential dancers are made more so by using their platform to share their voice and perspective. As a black woman and dancer of another generation, it was an honor to interview Michaela and see that she is using her talent to effect necessary changes and break down racial barriers.

made in sweden

more space in your life. more life in your space. string.se

string®

Stockists

& OTHER STORIES
stories.com

ACNE STUDIOS
acnestudios.com

A. F. VANDEVORST
afvandevorst.be

ALTA ORA
@alta_ora

ALTUZARRA
altuzarra.com

ANNE SOFIE MADSEN
annesofiemadsen.com

A.P.C.
apc.fr

APUNTOB
apuntob.com

ARNE JACOBSEN
arnejacobsenwatches.com

BAND OF OUTSIDERS
bandofoutsiders.com

BEHOMM
behomm.com

BORA AKSU
boraaksu.com

CALVIN KLEIN
calvinklein.com

CÉLINE
celine.com

COCLICO
coclico.com

CORNELIA WEBB
corneliawebb.com

COS
cosstores.com

DAVID LAPORT
davidlaport.com

DINNY HALL
dinnyhall.com

DRIES VAN NOTEN
driesvannoten.be

ERDEM
erdem.com

ERIK JØRGENSEN
erik-joergensen.com

FILLIPA K
filippa-k.com

FOE & DEAR
foeanddear.com

GOLDIE ROX
goldierox.com

GUCCI
gucci.com

HERMÈS
hermes.com

HERSCHEL
herschel.com

JW ANDERSON
j-w-anderson.com

JOHN LAWRENCE SULLIVAN
john-lawrence-sullivan.com

JOHN LOBB
johnlobb.com

KALLMEYER
kallmeyer.nyc

LOEWE
loewe.com

MACKINTOSH
mackintosh.com

MARGARET HOWELL
margarethowell.co.uk

MILK DECORATION
milkdecoration.com

MM6 MAISON MARGIELA
maisonmargiela.com

MOCKBERG WATCHES
mockberg.com

MORTEN USSING
mortenussing.com

MUUTO
muuto.com

PARACHUTE HOME
parachutehome.com

PAULA KNORR
paulaknorr.uk

PEET DULLAERT
peetdullaert.com

RAINS
rains.com

REJINA PYO
rejinapyo.com

RODEBJER
rodebjer.com

SCHOOLHOUSE
schoolhouse.com

SIMONE ROCHA
simonerocha.com

SOPHIE BILLE BRAHE
sophiebillebrahe.com

SOPHIE BUHAI
sophiebuhai.com

STRING
string.se

THE KOOPLES
thekooples.com

THE LINE
theline.com

TINA FREY
tinafreydesigns.com

TOGA ARCHIVES
toga.jp

VITRA
vitra.com

WOLF + RITA
wolfandrita.com

WOLFORD
wolford.com

XANDER ZHOU
xanderzhou.com

YOHJI YAMAMOTO
yohjiyamamoto.co.jp

**Behomm
Community**

Home Exchange for Creatives and Design Lovers

TRAVEL STAYING FOR FREE AT HOMES OF CREATIVES

1. REGISTER WITH YOUR HOME.
2. CONTACT A HOME YOU LIKE. AGREE ON DATES.
3. STAY AT THEIR HOME FOR FREE WHILE THEY STAY AT YOURS.

3100 MEMBERS IN 66 COUNTRIES   I   BEHOMM.COM

BEHOMM HOME ID 1231, PARIS

ISSUE 27

Credits

P.27
Courtesy of *Galerie Les Filles du Calvaire*

P.28
Top *Acne Studios*
Jacket *Vintage Yohji Yamamoto* from
James Veloria
Trousers *Vintage Gaultier* from *James Veloria*
Shoes *Kallmeyer*
Earrings *Alta Ora*

P.40
Photography Assistant
Abel Sloane

P.44
"Goodbye to All That" from
Slouching Towards Bethlehem
by *Joan Didion*
Copyright © 1966, 1968,
renewed 1996 by *Joan Didion*. Reprinted by
permission of the author.

P.64
Images courtesy of
Bureaux/Living Inside

P.74
Photography Assistant
Simon Thomsen

Makeup Assistant
Åsa Karlsten

Models
Ina Maribo, Lulu Leika & Leo Maribo at Scoop Models

P.114
Casting
Sarah Bunter

Photography Assistant
Carine Idy

Hair & Makeup Assistant
Leonor Greyl

Models
Kat at Studio KLRP
Elliot at PRM

P.166
Photograph:
Pierre Vauthey /Sygma/
Sygma via Getty Images

P.168—169
Photograph:
Jean-Claude Sauer/
Paris Match via
Getty Images

P.170
Photograph:
Reporters Associes/
Gamma-Rapho via
Getty Images

P.172—173
Photograph:
Jean-Claude Deutsch/
Paris Match via
Getty Images

P.174
Photograph:
Keystone-France/Gamma-
Rapho via Getty Images

P.176
Photograph:
*Jean-Claude Deutsch/*Paris
Match via Getty Images

Special Thanks
Mario Depicolzuane
Christian Møller Andersen
Sune at Scoop Models
Thejamjar Dubai